TALES, TELLERS AND TEXTS

Also available from Cassell:

Tales, Tellers and Texts

*Gabrielle Cliff Hodges, Mary Jane Drummond
and Morag Styles*

CASSELL

London and New York

Cassell

Wellington House   370 Lexington Avenue
125 Strand   New York
London WC2R 0BB   NY 10017–6550

First published 2000

British Library Cataloguing-in-Publication Data
A catalogue record for this book is available from the British Library.

ISBN 0–304–70641–8 (paperback)

Typeset by York House Typographic Ltd, London
Printed and bound in Great Britain by Biddles Ltd, www.Biddles.co.uk

Contents

The Contributors

Grant Bage worked as a teacher and adviser across a wide range of schools and curriculum areas before joining the School of Education, University of Cambridge, in 1995. He directs the TASTE [teaching as storytelling] Project, an inter-disciplinary initiative. He has recently led research for English Heritage and the Qualifications and Curriculum Authority (QCA) on the teaching and learning of history, and has been a writer and consultant for the BBC, HarperCollins*Publishers*, English Heritage and the British Library. As well as pursuing his lifelong interest in history and stories, he teaches and researches in the areas of curriculum leadership, teacher development and practitioner research.

Eve Bearne has taught English, drama and language in schools and colleges for over thirty years, and was a project officer for the National Writing Project. As editor or co-editor, she produced *Greater Expectations* (1995) and a series of books about children's literature, all published by Cassell. Her most recent publications focus on language and literacy: *Making Progress in English* (1998), *Use of Language in the Primary School* (1998) and *Use of Language across the Secondary School* (1999). She is Assistant Director of Research at Homerton College, Cambridge.

Gabrielle Cliff Hodges, formerly Head of English in a Cambridgeshire comprehensive school, is now a principal lecturer and secondary team leader at Homerton College, Cambridge. She has contributed chapters about poetry, speaking and listening to *Learning to Teach English in the Secondary School* (1997) and about the development of reading within the secondary age range to *Voices Off* (1996). She was chair of the National Association for the Teaching of English from 1996 to 1998.

Fiona Collins is a Research Associate based at Greenwich on the TASTE [teaching as storytelling] Project. She has a background in primary teaching and advisory work and is currently completing her PhD on oral storytelling. She has been a professional storyteller for nine years, working in a range of settings in Britain and abroad.

Kevin Crossley-Holland is renowned for his retelling of traditional tales, most notably in *The Penguin Book of Norse Myths*, *British Folk Tales* and *The Old Stories*. His translations of Anglo-Saxon poetry include *Beowulf* and *The Exeter Book of Riddles*, and he has written seven volumes of poetry, most recently *Poems From East Anglia*. His ghost story, *Storm*, won the 1985 Carnegie Medal. With Nicola LeFanu, he has written two operas based on traditional tales: *The Green Children* and *The Wildman*. He is currently working on a three-volume retelling of Arthurian legends for children and has recently been elected a Fellow of the Royal Society of Literature.

Jane Doonan is a leading critic who writes, reviews, teaches and lectures about illustrative art in picture books, combining aesthetic and semiotic approaches, as described in *Looking at Pictures in Picture Books* (Thimble Press, 1993). She has produced studies of some major picture-book makers and illustrators, including Tenniel, Zwerger, Kitamura and Sendak, as well as two surveys of Anthony Browne's work. She has contributed distinguished essays to the *Routledge International Encyclopedia of Children's Literature* (1996) and the forthcoming *Cambridge Guide to Children's Books*.

Mary Jane Drummond is a lecturer at the University of Cambridge School of Education, where she also researches in the field of early childhood education. Her abiding interest is in young children's learning; her book *Assessing Children's Learning* is published by David Fulton (1993).

Sarah Gordon is the author of a series of books on active approaches to Shakespeare in the primary school and also runs courses on the subject for teachers and inspectors. She is Artistic Director of Buttonhole Theatre Company and a freelance project trainer for a number of theatre companies, including Royal National Theatre, English Shakespeare Company, Orange Tree Theatre, Richmond and TAG Theatre Company, Glasgow. Her work in schools was recently the subject of a BBC Radio 4 documentary.

Judith Graham lectures at Roehampton Institute, London, and also at the School of Education, University of Cambridge. Previously she taught at the University of Greenwich and at the London Institute of Education. Her schoolteaching career was in London comprehensive schools. She is the author of *Pictures on the Page* (NATE, 1990) which discusses the role of illustration in children's literacy, and of *Cracking Good Books* (NATE, 1997), which is about teaching literature. *Cracking Good Picture Books* will be published in 1999. With co-author Alison Kelly, she has edited *Reading under Control* (David Fulton, 1997) and *Writing under Control* (David Fulton, 1998).

Tina L. Hanlon is an associate professor of English at Ferrum College and Hollins University Graduate Program in Children's Literature in Virginia, USA. She has published essays on folk tale adaptations, children's plays, picture books, Robinsonnades and environmental literature for children.

Hugh Lupton has worked as a professional storyteller for nearly twenty years. In 1985 he co-founded the highly influential Company of Storytellers. He has performed throughout Britain, as well as in North and South America, Europe and Africa, in thousands of venues. He has a particular passion for Greek, Celtic, Norse and Anglo-

Saxon mythological tales, for ballads and for the stories of his native East Anglia. Two collections of his retellings of traditional stories are published by Barefoot Books: *Tales of Wisdom and Wonder* (1998) and *Freaky Tales from Far and Wide* (1999).

Michael Rosen's first book for children, *Mind Your Own Business*, was published in 1974. Since then his prolific and popular output includes many collections of poetry and edited volumes of verse, as well as short stories, picture-book texts, adaptations of folk tales and a novel. For many years he presented *Treasure Islands*, BBC Radio 4's highly regarded programme about children's books. He currently presents *Word of Mouth*, a programme about language in use.

Morag Styles has lectured internationally on the teaching of literature, literacy and, particularly, poetry. Publications for Cassell include *From the Garden to the Street: 300 Years of Poetry for Children* (1998). She is also one of the co-editors of, and contributors to, a trilogy of texts on children's literature: *Voices Off* (1996), *The Prose and the Passion* (1994) and *After Alice* (1992). She is a Reader in Children's Literature and Language at Homerton College, Cambridge.

Frances Sword is Education Officer of the Fitzwilliam Museum, Cambridge, having previously worked at the Geffrye Museum, London. She also spent many years as a primary teacher, art tutor and artist. She has run many distinguished projects during her ten years at the Fitzwilliam Museum and worked with hundreds of schoolchildren and their teachers, as well as contributing to teacher education courses in Cambridge. Her innovative and inspirational teaching methods have been publicly recognized; awards and honours include Museum of the Year Award for the best educational initiative (1996) and a Churchill Travel Scholarship to study museum education in USA (1997).

David Whitley is a senior lecturer in English at Homerton College, Cambridge, where he teaches medieval literature, children's literature and media education. His research interests include 18th-century writing and media studies, particularly film. He has published extensively on Aesop's fables.

Acknowledgements

Every effort has been made to trace the copyright holders of material included in this book. However, the authors and publisher offer their apologies if any material has been included without permission, and will happily include appropriate acknowledgement in any future edition.

The illustrations in Chapter 7 from *Dragon Feathers* by Audrej Dugin and Olga Dugina are reproduced courtesy of Esslinger, Verlag J.F. Schreiber GmbH, Esslingen, Germany. Copyright © 1993 Esslinger Verlag J.F. Schreiber, Esslingen-Wien.

The illustrations in Chapter 9 from *Beware Beware*, written by Susan Hill, are reproduced by permission of the publisher Walker Books Limited, London. Illustrations © 1993 Angela Barrett.

This book is dedicated to the memory of

Eddie Steele Rosen
9 June 1980 – 27 April 1999

who was quite a teller himself
and loved a good tale

Introduction

Trafficking in Human Possibilities

Gabrielle Cliff Hodges

In recent centuries we speakers of this lovely language have reduced the English verb almost entirely to the indicative mood. But beneath that specious and arrogant assumption of certainty all the ancient, cloudy, moody powers and options of the subjunctive remain in force. The indicative points its bony finger at primary experiences, at the Things; but it is the subjunctive that joins them, with the bonds of analogy, possibility, probability, contingency, contiguity, memory, desire, fear and hope: the narrative connection.

(Le Guin, 1989)

THE PROLIFERATION OF NARRATIVES

As we stand on the brink of a new century it is tempting to remind ourselves of the sorts of predictions we have been making over the last hundred years and the extent to which they have been fulfilled. One commonly held view is that by now we would probably have witnessed the death of the book and seen it firmly replaced by the computer. Computers have certainly arrived but far from the bookless, high-tech society that science fiction writers and film makers have so often envisaged, we appear to be surrounded by more texts than ever. Likewise, many people predicted that we would find ourselves in an 'age of information' and that stories and narrative would have a much less important place. However, computer technology has itself created new and different ways of making, telling and sharing stories, resulting in even more narrative connections being made than ever before.

There is little doubt that the urge to tell and listen to stories is as powerful as ever. Our daily interactions with one another are punctuated by anecdotes which we use to inform each other, as well as to forge human relationships. In the workplace, in the pub, in the changing rooms, in the kitchen, in the classroom, we tell stories: the what and the why of day-to-day life, flavoured with different moral judgements; spiced with humour, sympathy, envy; leavened with speculation about future possibilities. Sometimes, however, a story needs more time and space for the telling. It may be a story which has been told and heard many times before, in which case it is not so much the story, but the manner of its telling that matters and gives pleasure, whether it be grandparents telling their grandchildren stories of their own childhood and youth, or professional story-tellers retelling traditional tales with a long and varied ancestry.

New technologies provide a multiplicity of ways to meet this need for narrative. Television, for example, is a major source. Its news programmes, chat shows, soaps, documentaries, wildlife programmes, serializations, dramas, films and advertisements provide a constant flow of narratives – some spontaneous, some carefully crafted – meeting a seemingly endless desire on the part of most of us to engage with, discuss and criticize them. Furthermore, television has generated new kinds of narratives uniquely suited to its relative intimacy and particular technology. Playwrights such as Stephen Poliakoff exploit the medium brilliantly, as in *Shooting the Past* (BBC, 1999), where many of the narratives which form the texture of the play are told through sequences of black-and-white photographs from the archives of the picture library in which it is set. On a different scale altogether is the *Rewind* series (BBC, 1999), currently being screened twice a week at the end of a children's television slot, working its way through each year of the century until the end of 1999. Here young people speak the words of their predecessors, retelling old stories in new voices, against a backdrop of archive footage: words taken from a diary written by a soldier during the First World War; the story of a woman's trip to Egypt where her father helped to discover the tomb of Tutenkhamun; and so on through the decades.

Radio, too, has provided countless opportunities for people to tell or hear stories. It is what people like to do. How else can we account for the enduring popularity of *The Archers*, or the readiness with which listeners submit their audio diaries to John Peel's library of *Home Truths*? Community radio and local television thrive on narrative, especially autobiography, biography and local history.

But perhaps the most extraordinary way in which narrative has proliferated is via the Internet. Despite inevitable anxieties about the adverse effects of this new technology it has, we now realize, opened up unforeseen opportunities. It is possible to gain access to people and their stories almost anywhere in the world, unimpeded by the usual gatekeepers of editors, publishing costs and so on. I can, for example, go in search of tales of the Blackfoot Nation and find myself on a personal website where someone has transcribed her grandmother's oral stories. Closer to home, I can find an account of a project in Cambridge for the National Year of Reading. A group of Bangladeshi women meet in their children's primary school over a period of weeks. There they tell traditional stories in Bengali, for example 'The Stork and the Tiger' and 'Seven Flower Brothers', translate them into English, illustrate them by means of a silk painting technique on squares of silk sewn into a quilt, then publish them on the Internet. Stories hitherto accessible to only a few, accompanied by pictures of the beautiful quilted squares, become accessible to anyone, anywhere via the National Year of Reading website. Likewise, the millennium *Schoolnet 2000* project invites young people to gather narratives – autobiographical, historical or fictional – from their families and communities throughout the country and add them to what may turn out to be an extraordinary electronic *Doomsday Book*. The Internet offers a special democratic freedom for personal narratives. We cannot yet know what the full effect of this technological capability will be, either on those who use it to publish or those who read what is there. In the meantime, however, it seems to have bolstered the reading of traditional print texts, either through virtual booksellers or through websites related to series titles, authors, playwrights and poets. The success of TV and film tie-in publishing is further evidence of how the power and pleasures of different technologies – this time the moving image – generate a desire for print versions, whether poetry (Auden's 'Funeral Blues' in *Four Weddings and a Funeral*), drama (Baz Luhrman's *Romeo and Juliet*), non-fiction (*Titanic*) or novels (*Pride and Prejudice*; *Madame Doubtfire*).

However, newspapers, magazines, comics, graphic novels and books, in their own right, remain a staple in many people's reading diets, for children and adults alike. Millions enjoy popular forms of narrative whether via *Just 17*, a *Goosebumps* book, the pages of *The Sun*, a novel by Jeffrey Archer. Sales point undeniably to a craving for this variety of reading pleasures. It seems, therefore, that narrative and storytelling are very much alive and well: old forms hold their own but make room for new ones alongside them.

Nevertheless, a computer with its screen, sound card, and mouse is a different physical object from a book. It hums, it is on the move, it scrolls down its graphics, it clears them at a click. These facilities have their advantages, but we must remember that a screen image of a silk quilt is not an adequate substitute for its actual soft, smooth textures, its rich colours, its gold edging; electronic print, however attractive, cannot replace a human voice, speaking, storytelling, reading. We need plenty of opportunities to hear the nuances and intonation of different narrative voices in order to make them sound for us in our own retellings, our own silent readings. These are the voices we hear, especially in carefully crafted tellings, whether by parent, teacher or professional storyteller, tellings designed and shaped to entertain, to teach, to be remembered and passed on.

They are also the voices we hear when written texts are read aloud. A century and a half ago Charles Dickens mesmerized his audiences at his public readings because he knew the dramatic potential of narrative, especially when brought to life by the speaking voice. To help him, he used to mark his prompt copies with stage directions. In his copy of *A Christmas Carol*, at the words 'Once upon a time – of all the good days in the year, upon a Christmas Eve – old Scrooge sat busy in his counting house ... ' he wrote the word *Narrative*. He knew the phrase 'Once upon a time' would draw in his audience. But he knew the importance of prosody as well. Rowland Hill, a journalist who attended Dickens's readings of *A Christmas Carol*, made extensive notes on how he achieved his effects. At this point, he tells us, Dickens 'chang(ed) his tone suddenly to a rich mellow note, splendidly inflected' (Collins, 1983).

FACT AND FANCY

Given Dickens's passion for narrative, it is not surprising to find him, in *Hard Times*, speculating on what might happen if we tried to stick to the factual and to wean ourselves off tale-telling. His firm conclusion is that Thomas Gradgrind's philosophy of 'nothing but facts' is unsustainable. Fancy, imagination and the old stories are as essential to human beings as breathing, and have to survive. It is hard for the factual to exist without the imaginative. We perceive, as Valentine Cunningham puts it, 'the impossibility of maintaining hedges between the Circus and the Factory'. Dickens's actual writing in *Hard Times*, Cunningham points out, is immersed in both the literal and the figural, the worldly and the textual. And, in fact, whatever pole of that bipolarity is repressed or devalued, it has a tendency to return, to resurface, to insist on its co-presence in the texture of the whole.

(Cunningham, 1994)

The interplay between these poles gives narrative its unique momentum, its dynamic force which may help to account for its enduring popularity as a genre, and for the recent identification of 'faction' – fiction based upon true stories – as a strong favourite. Perhaps, as Harold Rosen proposes:

Inside every non-narrative kind of discourse there stalk the ghosts of narrative and ... inside every narrative there stalk the ghosts of non-narrative discourse.

(Rosen, 1985)

Recent arguments amongst those concerned with the education of young people have increasingly pushed other genres than the narrative to the forefront. Much attention has been focused, for example, on non-fiction and the need to raise its profile in the English curriculum. New research (Hall and Coles, 1999) supports the need for a move in this direction but reveals, nevertheless, that narrative remains a dominant *book*-reading preference. Amongst not just girls, but boys as well, the most popular types of book are narratives – adventure and horror stories, to be precise. However, magazines, comics and newspapers are also widely read, and read predominantly as informational texts. But even here, narratives play an important part:

There is, in the most popular periodicals, factual information, for example about real aspects of sports culture, but there is also a fictionalised element constituted by the particular placement of the reader in relation to sports heroes and pop stars, who are often portrayed in a way which feeds the imagination and fantasies of young readers. Invented stories from 'facts' are an increasing element in our culture ... Many boys' enjoyment of narrative is perhaps via this genre of invented stories from facts, particularly in magazines.

(Hall and Coles, 1999)

In girls' magazines, likewise, in addition to the abundance of information they contain, there are also stories which are presented

swiftly and succinctly, with an emphasis on plot and accounts of emotion. The predominant literary form is heightened realism which places considerable emphasis on the apparent authenticity of experience.

(*ibid.*)

Many people, therefore, seem to enjoy this middle position, this combination of fact and fancy, even if they also seek pleasure in one or the other separately from time to time.

ACTIVE OR PASSIVE?

Reading, viewing or listening to narrative means not just weaving a way between the worldly and the imagined. It means actively bringing together a multiplicity of skills: textual decoding, interpretation and criticism. Watching films or reading popular fiction sometimes conjures up an image of passivity, but this begins to fade when we understand more fully what is involved in different narratives and consider them critically. Narratives, in whatever medium, make considerable intellectual, linguistic and social demands on the producer: to take into account the audience; to place in sequence and to layer ideas and events; to establish and sustain characterization; to use the medium with fluency and accuracy (Wood, 1988). They involve an equally complex set of intellectual procedures on the part of the receiver. Perhaps it is precisely because of the exertions necessary in apprehending as well as making stories that so many find the experience pleasurable, rewarding and motivating. Nevertheless, some people remain uneasy about privileging narrative over other genres, especially within the school curriculum. Peter Medway, for example, has suggested that

> Many fiction-based assignments . . . absolve [students] from the work of ascribing meaning to the world, implying that only fictional worlds have identifiable order and signifi-cance.
>
> (Medway, 1988)

His argument is that when students work with narrative they are divorced from their real lives and trapped within a genre which does not allow them to be critical interrogators of the world in which they live. If, however, like Ursula Le Guin, we take the view that fictional or literary narratives offer opportunities to operate in the subjunctive rather than the indicative mood, then their emancipatory potential may become clearer. In *Actual Minds, Possible Worlds* (1986) Bruner explores two distinct, complementary modes of thought – story and argument – and suggests that those who deal in narratives do not do so in order to know the truth, so much as to explore the meaning of experiences. To that end narrators privilege the hypothetical over and above the factual. They offer the experience of 'trafficking in human possibilities rather than in settled certainties' (Bruner, 1986). The word 'trafficking' brings into play all sorts of dynamic images: of to-ing and fro-ing across borders and boundaries; of subversion and double-dealing; of brokering and bartering, mediation and exchange; of pleasure and satisfaction; of risk and danger. Traffickers are sometimes working for those who are more powerful than them, but sometimes they control operations themselves. Either way, if fictional worlds have about them the aura of the possible, then they offer a chance to reflect on the actual without being entirely bound by it. In this way, they have the potential to be emancipatory.

DEALERS IN NARRATIVE

In 1994 considerable controversy surrounded the Carnegie Award being won by Robert Swindells for his chilling novel *Stone Cold*. Its dual first person narrative tells the intertwined stories of a homeless teenager on the streets and a serial killer. Adults who condemned it seemed to be ignoring the processes involved in creating narratives, whether as reader, listener, writer or viewer: the steering of a path between the real and the fictional; the engaging with a text to explore the human possibilities however grim or fantastic; the disengagement afterwards in order to gain critical distance. Although they are not always aware of it, adults and children do apprehend narratives like this. Evidence is provided in the exchanges which follow between a teacher and a group of Year 7 students about their story reading, writing and dramatization, even if they struggle to articulate it (Cliff Hodges, 1990). First, their story writing:

Teacher: Do you use your own lives?
Dean: I just make things up about my Dad and me ... doing things
Teacher: So when you write you are in your own stories?
Dean: Yeah ... it's mostly me and my dad in my stories.
Jane: Some stories, if they're like mysteries and that, I'm making them up.
Mandy: But sometimes it's not me but I'm acting one of the other people but it's not actually as me.
Dean: You're doing your own piece but you're not ... you're doing your own piece but you've got a different name instead of your own name.
Teacher: What about when you write these stories about you and your dad – do you write about things you've actually done or things you would like to do?
Dean: Would like to do. If my mum and dad were still together.

Dean is under no illusions, however. About reading he says:

Dean: If something's really bad [in stories] it always turns out right but in real life if something's bad it turns – it keeps going bad, doesn't it ... You wish for something and it never happens ... The best things don't and the really horrible things do.

That doesn't stop him or his peers from engaging in the practices of narrative and enjoying themselves. Another student explains something of the particular pleasure:

Brian: My stories are usually long consisting of eight pages with illustrations. I get ideas from what I would like to happen to myself.
Teacher: When you're writing your own stories like these ... where do your ideas come from?
Brian: Well ... I have what I'd like to be. What I'd like my character ... what I want to be but I can't be ... I want it to be me but I can't 'cos where I live ... the way I live changes it ... I want to live in a big old farmhouse out in the country with ... like an old shed of my own and everything in it of my own ... I'd like to be sort of like a secret detective and have my own sort of group ...
Teacher: Group of detectives?
Brian: I can have my own private place and keep it secret ... and live in the middle of nowhere.

In the dramatic narratives which students create, they are equally capable of emotional engagement with plot, setting and character, of entering into the dramatic space without losing the capacity to retrace their steps. One such drama, created over a period of several weeks, involved the imaginative construction of a village from which the inhabitants were to be evicted so that the area could be flooded to form a reservoir. In the final lesson, students were in role as villagers revisiting the place many years later when a hot rainless summer has left the reservoir dried out. Later, out of role, they were asked to comment on their work. The language of their explanations demonstrates the fine dividing line between imaginative engagement and critical distance:

Neil: When we walked out of our house I felt sad because we have been in it all through the story and after forty years when we came back it seemed strange as if we'd never known the place.

Daniel: We were looking at nothing that was nothing in the first place … Well, [the village] was what we made up and really it was nothing. Then we had to dream [it] as if *it* was nothing. It was just ruins … we were supposed to be looking at nothing which was in real life nothing.

What Daniel attempts to articulate is the 'reality' of the imagination, the simultaneous 'being' and 'not being' that is the narrative process. One might suppose that reading or viewing would be more all-absorbing than writing or performing; because the craft or design is someone else's business the receiver is the more deluded. Perhaps so, on the surface. But, again, students who are asked to explain what is going on when they read, remarkably find ways to explain it, none better than in the example below. A Year 10 class had been reading *Jane Eyre*. They had just finished the episode in the Red Room in which the following passage occurs:

I had to cross before the looking-glass; my fascinated glance involuntarily explored the depth it revealed. All looked colder and darker in that visionary hollow than in reality: and the strange little figure there gazing at me, with a white face and arms specking the gloom, and glittering eyes of fear moving where all else was still, had the effect of a real spirit.

(Brontë, 1966)

The power of the 'visionary hollow' of narrative to produce sensations which are more intense than reality, can allow a fictional character, too, to have 'the effect of a real spirit'. One student wrote in her reading journal how her mind was working as she read this particular passage. She explained that she felt as if she herself was approaching the mirror, she herself was looking into the mirror but what she saw was Jane's face, not her own, looking back at her. Jane sees a spirit, not herself; the student saw Jane, not herself. Jane, the spirit/reflection and the student are simultaneously linked and distinct: the narrative connection.

These examples of students reflecting on the processes of narrative provide a glimpse of the complexities of the form and the different dimensions in which participants operate as they craft new worlds, enact human possibilities, perform rather than recite the texts that others have already made. If dealing in narrative involves all these operations, then it would seem to be a very rich domain for learning, a very important alternative way to explore, to know, to feel, to understand. The examples also make clear how a critical stance provides a solid defence against seduction. Despite the powerful imaginative pull, the reader, listener or viewer remains very firmly in control.

Most people, especially young people, like to feel in control. Here, then, may be another reason for the continuing popularity of narrative.

BORDERS AND BOUNDARIES

A particular source of interest in many narratives is that in order to be worth the telling they deal with difference, with life at border crossings. We engage with characters momentarily poised on the brink and are motivated by our curiosity to know what happens. Characters veer between oppositions, positioned often between two states: childhood/adulthood; inside/outside; reality/fantasy; good/evil. The narrative offers a chance not only to explore alternatives but also an invitation to arbitrate. Although they may begin with what *is*, they move to what *if*.

Take Tony Mitton's narrative poem *The Seal Hunter* (Mitton, 1998), for example. It is a modern retelling in poetry of a selkie story which begins with things as they are but moves to things as they might be. A greedy seal-hunter is drawn by a stranger down into the world of the seals. Beneath the water, the hunter expects to drown. But this is story. The hunter (like the reader) finds that he can live in a different medium:

> And down in that weird and greeny light
> where he thought to meet his death,
> when his will gave way and he drank the brine
> he found he could draw his breath.
>
>   (Mitton, 1998)

The seals, furthermore, speak with him, confronting him with his greed for their pelts. Although the reader is exploring imaginary worlds where a man can survive under water and seals can speak, the moral point is firmly anchored in human reality. The literal and the figural coincide. The reader becomes a witness, one who sees (literally one who knows), one who is present at the trial. Eventually, the hunter takes the selkie vow: to guard, not to plunder what lives in the sea, and as he does so, the darkness seems to gather round and wrap him like cloak:

> He fell into a deep sea swoon
> where waters rolled him round.
> And when he woke it seemed to him
> he lay on solid ground.
>
>   (*ibid.*)

This narrative experience (within and without the poem) is what Seamus Heaney describes in *The Redress of Poetry* as 'the imagination pressing back against the pressure of reality' (Heaney, 1995), an experience which can produce a scintillating friction. Although he is referring to poetry, Heaney's description of this process can equally be applied to story:

> Such an operation does not intervene in the actual but by offering consciousness a chance
> to recognise its predicaments, foreknow its capacities and rehearse its comebacks in all

kinds of venturesome ways, it does constitute a beneficent event, for poet and audience alike. It offers a response to reality which has a liberating and verifying effect upon the individual spirit.

(ibid.)

Heaney thus acknowledges that although such crafting of events may not in itself be productive of new events, it offers a position from which to reflect upon actual experience, and perhaps be made different as a result.

CRITICAL NARRATIVES

Critical awareness of narrative comes partly from being taught explicitly about it within a formal educational context. Partly, though, it comes from engaging with critical narratives, those which entice you out onto the margins where there are risks to take, where the going may be tough, where there are crucial decisions to be made, where you are invited to witness, even deal in, an array of human possibilities. Those who craft stories, whether storytellers, novelists, picture storybook writers and artists, film makers, playwrights, poets, hypertext creators, acknowledge and develop this adventurousness in the narratives they produce. They can operate at the boundaries of readers' previous achievements and lead them on ever more exciting expeditions. The reward is for readers to experience the press of imagination against reality; the challenge of metaphor, grammar, syntax, structure; the multiplicity of voices. One result may be the chance to make new sense of human experience.

Many such critical narratives, old and new, form the subject of this book, which arose from a joint project in Cambridgeshire (supported by Homerton College, Cambridge University School of Education, Cambridgeshire County Council and Cambridge University Press) to mark the National Year of Reading in the UK in 1999. We needed 'no ghost from the grave' to urge upon us the importance of stories and reading, but a publication offered us the opportunity to extend the work of the project beyond its geographical boundaries and the Year of Reading itself.

The book is divided into four sections, the first of which focuses on oral narratives. Kevin Crossley-Holland explores the subtle links and distinctions between oral and written storytelling, describing the skill and craft involved as well as the storyteller's many responsibilities, especially to young audiences. Hugh Lupton, like Kevin Crossley-Holland, shows how his work provides narrative connections between the here-and-now and the most ancient of tales and tellers, via the footpaths of oral traditions throughout the world. In the final part of this section, Grant Bage explores the role of the teacher as a storyteller, someone who can use narrative as a powerful force for learning.

An account of storytelling in the classroom begins Section Two on historical narratives. Fiona Collins describes how fragments of local history can be crafted into stories, drawing on and extending children's understanding of both history and narrative in the process. Judith Graham reconsiders historical novels for children, analysing recent examples of the genre to demonstrate some of the richly imaginative ways in which writers construct a sense of historical period and appeal to a contemporary readership. We come, finally, to retellings of one of the most popular narrative cycles of all time: Chaucer's *Canterbury Tales*, perhaps some of the most complex, multi-layered narratives of them all. What, asks David Whitley, do new versions of the tales offer today's young readers? To what extent do children's experiences match what scholars and adult readers have always found most valuable and stimulating in Chaucer's work?

Section Three concerns visual narratives. Two of its chapters, one by Jane Doonan and one by Tina Hanlon, explore in illuminating detail the complexities of the picture storybook. They remind us of the intellectual interactions between the reader, the artist and the writer. Their analyses challenge any notions of pictorial narratives as simplistic or undemanding. Frances Sword considers the narrative potential of artefacts and paintings in the context of museums and galleries. She describes how inviting young people to make narrative connections between what they can see and the knowledge they bring with them, can lead, under the imaginative guidance of the teacher, to further hypothesis and speculation, activities which mirror the work of archaeologists, art historians, and all those who engage in similar detective work. It also leads to children's own narratives.

In the fourth section the authors consider a range of literary narratives. Sarah Gordon looks at stories from Shakespeare as they are re-enacted in primary classrooms four centuries on from their inception. Mary Jane Drummond revisits the work of a 19th-century writer of prose fiction, George Macdonald, focusing on his understanding of the nature of imagination and its importance in children's lives. She argues that Macdonald's greatness as a writer of fairy stories lies in his appreciation of children's powers to feel, to understand and to do good, and his determination to feed and exercise those powers. In the final chapter in this section, Michael Rosen considers that most important and sometimes elusive figure, the narrator, in particular the first-person narrator. Reflecting on various phases in his own poetry writing, he uncovers different 'I's in different poems and speculates on their origins.

Lastly, there are the newest narratives, those which the latest technologies have made possible. Eve Bearne closes the book with an examination of some of these new texts and the new ways of reading with which so many young people are now familiar. Rightly, she urges all of us who are involved with young people to learn for ourselves about such texts and technologies, to consider how to intervene productively at the points where texts and young readers meet to ensure that they are equipped not only to engage in the deep pleasures that new narratives offer but to know how and why they work.

REFERENCES

Brontë, C. (1966) *Jane Eyre*. London: J.M. Dent and Sons Ltd.

Bruner, J. (1986) *Actual Minds, Possible Worlds*. Cambridge, Massachusetts: Harvard University Press.

Cliff Hodges, G. (1990) *Using Narrative Texts in Secondary Schools*. Unpublished dissertation in part fulfilment of the MA in Language and Literature in Education, Institute of Education, University of London.

Collins, P. (ed.) (1983) *Charles Dickens: Sikes and Nancy and Other Public Readings*. Oxford: Oxford University Press.

Cunningham, V. (1994) *In the Reading Gaol: Postmodernity, Texts and History*. Oxford: Blackwell.

Hall, C. and Coles, M. (1999) *Children's Reading Choices*. London: Routledge.

Heaney, S. (1995) *The Redress of Poetry*. London: Faber & Faber.

Le Guin, U. (1989) *Dancing at the Edge of the World*. London: Victor Gollancz.

Medway, P. (1988) 'The Students' World and the World of English', in *English in Education*, Vol. 22, No. 2, NATE.

Mitton, T. (1998) *The Seal Hunter*. London: Scholastic Children's Books.

Rosen, H. (1985) *Stories and Meanings*. Sheffield: NATE.

Wood, D. (1988) *How Children Think and Learn*. Oxford: Blackwell.

I

Oral Narratives

Chapter 1

Different – But Oh How Like!

Kevin Crossley-Holland

In his poem 'Yes, it was the Mountain Echo', William Wordsworth has the line 'Like – but oh how different!' The voice and echo, he says, the oral source and its repetition, are less similar than dissimilar.

Well, maybe! But as one reflects on what responsibilities oral storytellers and writers may have, and what strategies they may devise, one may well conclude that it is not a matter of 'Like – but oh how different!' but, rather, 'Different – but oh how like!' So that, with apologies to Mr Wordsworth, is the title of this chapter.

What I have to say falls into five unequal parts: first an attempt at a redefinition of traditional tale; then some brief comments on accounts of storytelling; so into the meat of the matter with a discussion of the storyteller's responsibilities; and of ways of retelling tales I have found fruitful; finally, a few remarks on the educational uses of tale.

To my mind, a traditional tale may be a myth or a folk tale and is in either case a metaphor which entertains and instructs: a narrative in the first instance oral, which is the product of no single person, place or time, and which has been retuned and sometimes reclothed by those who have transmitted it.

A myth is a story within a loosely knit cycle of narratives which together amount to a sacred history. This history is panoptic. It assigns human beings their place within the entire order of creation, but its first matter is not women or men but their giant shadows, the goddesses and gods. Myth looks back, myth looks forward, myth explains and warns. Always, it is concerned with the welfare of women and men not only as social animals but as spiritual beings.

A folk tale is the generic term for many different kinds of narrative, always brief enough to be digested at one sitting. The cast of thousands consists of humans, animals and supernatural beings of all kinds (as well as talking plants, trees and natural phenomena), but never the celestial beings who created them. The character of folk tale is direct narrative, in which the emphasis is on action as opposed to idea or feeling, and its purpose is to illustrate the whole gamut of non-religious human experience – all the longings and rewards and sorrows and frustrations and hazards and absurdities of our lives.

The folk tale tree is laden with fruit of many shapes, sizes and colours: etiological (or aetiological) tales that inhabit the borders of myth as they explain origins and causes – how, for example, the body of the Muckle Mester Stoor Worm turned into the islands of Orkney and Shetland and Faroe and Iceland; tales of fabulous beasts -Jacqueline Simpson tells us there are more than one hundred villages in Britain with their own distinct dragon stories; tales of shape-changers; giant stories; stories of heroes and strong men, and saints and devils (Simpson, 1980). Then there are fairy tales, involving supernatural beings and magic; it is incorrect to speak of 'folk and fairy tales' as two genres, for the latter is simply one species of the former; there are wonder tales; jocular tales; fables; nursery tales.

In addition to these categories, there is that kind of tale in which a moment of definable or indefinable historical actuality is embedded within any amount of fantastic invention. Most ghost stories belong in this category. And so do those stories we call legends, or folk legends.

How is it that Richard Whittington, philanthropic Lord Mayor of London, became hero of a tale in which his cat made his fortune on the Barbary coast? And how come the 13th-century abbot of a Cistercian monastery at Coggeshall describes a wildman, a sort of marine woodwose, and the way in which he was hoicked out of the sea by fishermen at Orford in Suffolk?

What actually happened? In such tales, what is fact, what fiction, and how did they come to combine? These are the fascinating and largely unanswerable questions always begged by legend.

I sometimes think it is useful to think of a legend in this way. An oyster gets a piece of grit inside its shell. 'Ugh!', it says, or slobbers, or whatever oysters do. 'Ugh! My shoulder's itching!' So what does this oyster do about it? It exudes its own balm, it surrounds the source of its itch with that nacreous substance we call pearl. Likewise, a legend has at its heart a piece of grit: a moment of historical substance. Around it there gathers and grows an accretion, the filaments of imagination. Grit and invention: together they form the pearl of legend.

Will you step for a moment into your early childhood? The village or street where you lived. Is there anyone living nearby whom you, and maybe your friends, suppose about, talk about, maybe even worry about? Is he really a werewolf? Is she a witch?

Most of us can think of such a person, someone who set our imagination racing, someone we have continued to think of from time to time, adding and subtracting to and from the persona, part fact and part fantasy, that we created years ago.

In the seaside village in north Norfolk where I spent my holidays as a boy, just a mile away from where I now live, there was a woman called Sheila Disney. She had slightly webbed fingers and webbed feet. I think she did! Anyhow, she told me once she was descended from a seal, and I saw no reason to disbelieve her. After all, I knew that Shetlandic tale about a seal-woman who marries a fisherman, and gives birth to human children. But Miss Disney – everyone called her Diz – also told me she was an eastern, English cousin of the great Walt! I think she did. And she had a moustache! This seal-woman barked, and she scared me stupid; she taught me to swim, after a fashion; and wading along the muddy creek, she used to catch her breakfast – some luckless passing flatfish – with her feet. Not so long ago, I wrote a verse about her:

Easterlies have sandpapered her larynx.

Webbed fingers, webbed feet:

last child of a seal family.

There is a blue flame at her hearth, blue
mussels at her board.
Her bath is the gannet's bath.

Rents one windy room at the top of a ladder.
Reeks of kelp.

'Suffer the little children,' she barks,
and the children – all the little ones –
are enchanted.

She has stroked through the indigo of
Dead Man's Pool
and returned with secrets.

They slip their moorings. They
tack towards her glittering eyes.

(Crossley-Holland, 1997a)

You see? A hopeless mixture! Memory of actuality *and* deliberate invention which, at this late date, can scarcely be separated. This is what legend is; and you and I, we have all created our own legends.

There is nothing so fascinating as coming to grips with process, whether it be watch-making or furniture-making, bellringing or learning to fly. And when that process is one we have attempted ourselves, we compare, we learn, and we enjoy a sense of almost conspiratorial intimacy. That is why I often go back to accounts by folklorists of the oral storyteller in action:

> Her memory kept a firm grip on all the stories. She herself knew that this gift was not granted to everyone, and that there were many who could remember nothing con-nectedly. She told her stories thoughtfully, accurately, with wonderful vividness, and evidently had delight in doing so.
>
> (Dorson, 1968)

That is how Jacob and Wilhelm Grimm described a village woman from near Kassel who provided them with a number of tales during the first decade of the 19th-century.

My second storyteller is the redoubtable Peig Sayers, who lived on the Blasket Islands until they were evacuated in the 1930s. She recorded many tales on Ediphone cylinders and, in the words of Seósamn Ó Daleigh:

> Great artist and wise woman that she was, Peig would at once switch from gravity to gaiety, for she was a light-hearted woman, and her changes of mood and face were like the changes of running water. As she talked her hands would be working too: a little slap of the palms to cap a phrase, a flash of the thumb over her shoulder to mark a mystery, a hand hushed to mouth for mischief or whispered secrecy.
>
> (O'Sullivan, 1996)

The last of my accounts was written by John Francis Campbell of Islay. He and his team of Gaelic speakers collected no fewer than 791 tales (there are 86 in his four-volume *Popular Tales of the West Highlands*, 1860–62), and in this vivid passage he sets the storyteller in context:

> One woman was industriously weaving in a corner, another was carding wool, and a girl was spinning dextrously with a distaff made of a rough-forked birch-branch, and a spindle which was little better than a splinter of fir. In the warm nook behind the fire sat a girl with one of those strange foreign faces which are occasionally to be seen in the Western Isles, and which are often supposed by their neighbours to mark the descendants of the Spanish crews of the wrecked Armada ... Old men and young lads, newly returned from the eastern fishing, sat about on benches fixed to the wall, and smoked and listened; and Macdonald sat on a low stool in the midst, and chanted forth his lays amid suitable remarks and ejaculations of praise and sympathy. One of the poems was the 'Lay of Diarmaid' ... 'Och! och! – aw! is not that sad?' said the women when Diarmaid was expiring.
>
> (Dorson, 1968)

Now let me isolate and slightly expand the qualities ascribed to these storytellers:

memory: that is to say the establishing of the storyteller as part of the tradition through reliable recall; anything less sows seeds of doubt; and each story has its own sequence, shape and proportions as surely as an egg-timer has a waist;

thoughtfulness: the storyteller cares for and gives proper weight to each character and action; he or she – I think I will settle for she – is involved in a tale but may also stand outside it and comment on it;

accuracy: mastery of language; no action or thought or feeling or description is greater than the language which expresses it;

vividness: the use of words to make memorable images and memorable sounds;

constant changes of mood: a folk tale is always fast on its feet and embodies a wide range of emotion;

use of face and hands: while words tell a story, expression and gesture enact it;

and finally, **delight**: delight in story and delight in the art of storytelling; delight in the act of sharing which, as Jack Zipes says in *Revisiting the Storyteller*, awakens the storyteller in others and is an act of liberation (Zipes, 1996).

In these short passages, then, there are valuable lessons for oral storytellers and writers alike, as well as indications of some of the elements that separate them.

In a preliterate society, it is customary for the poet and storyteller to undergo formal training. How else can she become guardian of the memory-hoard? In Heroic Age Ireland, for instance, the *filid* served an apprenticeship of seven years; doubtless he learned from existing practitioners about the very qualities we have just isolated; and he was expected to commit to memory more than 250 tales.

The contemporary storyteller is no longer the living memory of the tribe, unless she is one of the tiny minority who belong to a preliterate society; but for all that, she has responsibilities, and not only those implied in the passages by Grimm, Ó Daleigh and Campbell.

To begin with, storytellers – no matter how substantial or modest their aims – will do well to spend some time inhabiting the world of traditional tale: only when they win a decent working knowledge of the canon and can proceed on the basis of comparison – comparison of different motifs, comparison of the same motif from different sources – can they feel fully confident in their choice of matter. And only when they are fully aware of the remarkable amount of leaves on the storytree will they be likely to choose little-known material instead of playing 'follow my leader'. It is encouraging that so very many anthologies of folk tales have been published during the last generation, but discouraging that relatively few break substantial new ground in their choice of tale.

I do not mean that we should not engage with and renew 'standards' such as 'Cinderella' (in one of its more than 300 versions!), 'Sleeping Beauty' and 'Jack and the Beanstalk'. Of course we should. They are tales with unsurpassable characterization and colour, movement and meaning. What I am saying is that there are very many other great tales that are scarcely known at all, and that they present storytellers both with opportunity and responsibility.

Of their nature, folk tales reconcile people of different gender, colour, race and nation. Their ground is what humans hold in common, not what divides them. But although many tales may share one motif, the flesh and clothing of each varies greatly from the others, and depends on local circumstance. It follows that the storyteller's second responsibility is, like the first, contextual.

It is scarcely adequate to select and retell or rewrite a tale without having some knowledge of the culture from which that tale comes. With such knowledge, the reteller is likely to avoid a number of obvious traps: the misunderstanding of idea, behaviour or terminology; the exoticising of the humdrum; and the reinforcing of divisive cultural and national stereotypes.

Let the storyteller be assured, on the other hand, that traditional tale is indeed a *jeu sans frontières*, and that desirable sensitivity to cultural difference is not to be confused with political correctness, which is reductive and stupid. I give little credence to the notion that, because I am a man and white and Anglo-Saxon (a deadly trio!) I may not give words in a tale to, say, an Aboriginal or Inuit woman, on the grounds that I can have no imaginative empathy with her condition. That way lies madness. Are Othello and Porgy and Bess and Madam Butterfly to be chucked on to the scrapheap? It is absurd to argue that an artist can speak for no-one but himself.

I think the storyteller's third responsibility is to the chosen tale. Before she reshapes it, she must enter it and allow it to enter her. What does the tale say? What does it mean? Does it have more than one meaning? More than two? And if the tale originated in a known place and moment, as is likely with legend, what did it mean to its original audience? What parts of the action are structural and what incidental? Which words of which characters are crucial and which casual?

Only when the teller has really pondered questions of this kind can she feel free to remake it. And of course, in exercising this freedom, the teller may well choose to change the emphasis of a tale so that it speaks to her own time and society.

Take, for example, the popular 15th-century Norfolk tale of 'The Pedlar of Swaffham': the account of a man who has a dream, and walks halfway across England because of it, only to learn of gold buried in his backyard – a fortune he dedicates to the rebuilding of the local church. Is this story about divine purpose – the way in which absolutely everything that happens is part of God's plan? Is it about the advisability of buying a ticket to heaven? Is it concerned with the importance of dream and intuition? Is it about the value of dogged persistence? Is it about how the greatest treasure is not to be found far afield but on our own doorsteps? Storytellers divided by more than 500 years might very well come to different conclusions about the meaning of such a tale. But provided the contemporary storyteller has carefully questioned the source, and does not arbitrarily impose but elicits and develops meanings, there is nothing whatsoever wrong with that.

The storyteller's fourth responsibility is to craft and language. She must try to find a shape appropriate to meaning, cultural origin, audience, and she must try to find the right words to tell or write the tale. No easy task! I'll confine myself here to a few comments on language, and say something later about craft in relation to my own storytelling strategies.

The language of folk tale, like the action of folk tale, is not complicated or fatty: it is simple and lean. This is because it derives from the oral tradition; because it deals in actions always, and seldom in feelings or ideas; and because it aims to speak to a wide, often unlearned and often youthful audience. The words in our language that describe things, not ideas and feelings, very largely derive from Anglo-Saxon. Womb (*wamb*), man (*mon*), child (*cild*), water (*waeter*), earth (*eorthe*), plough (*ploh*), root (*rot*) – the very fabric of life. The language of folk tale retold in English must surely come from this root too: words that are quick and clean and taut and true. Short words pack the greatest punch.

In the same spirit, the language of folk tale will be rich in nouns and adjectives but have little time for adverbs; sometimes I think we could do without adverbs altogether. And it will not be slowed and sargassoed in a sea of passive verbs; rather, good retellings live and kick in the present and active tense.

The canon of traditional tale; the culture to which a tale belongs; the chosen tale itself; and craft and language: above and beyond these four considerations, oral and literary storytellers share one further responsibility, and that is to their audience.

As their name implies, traditional tales usually have their own histories, and have survived for generations, though I'm aware, of course, of the body of urban legends, such as 'The Hook' and 'The Vanishing Hitchhiker' and 'The Runaway Grandmother', which are of comparatively recent vintage.

The chief reason why early 19th-century European antiquarian and social historians began to write down traditional tales – the trickle of curiosity soon becoming a floodtide of fascination – was because they witnessed the dislocations of the Industrial Revolution. As families moved from green country to black country (what a depth charge those two words have when set side by side!), and from village to city, so as to sustain and develop the manufacturing industries, they leeched and fractured rural communities in a way not seen since the dreadful plagues of the 14th-century. The arrival of mechanized travel, the growth of literacy, penny newspapers, gas lighting: they too all played a part in undermining family and village as integrated, self-sustaining and self-entertaining units to which more than ninety per cent of the population belonged.

Jacob and Wilhelm Grimm were the first to appreciate the implications of this earthquake, and to set down tales as they heard them from rural folk in Saxony during the first decade of the 19th-century, for fear they would otherwise be completely forgotten and lost. Since the brothers Grimm and most of those who followed them into the field were recording what was essentially a rural tradition, it is not surprising that, when the tales they set down had a setting to speak of (and many folk tales do not), it was a rural one. Neither is it surprising that when those tales were set in a specific time (and most are not), that time was often generations or centuries before the 19th-century. In such static and conservative communities, everyone knew one another and knew every grassblade of gossip, and people only ventured into the local market town, on foot or in a cart, two or three times a year. Time came 'dropping slow', and memory was extended and savoured. 'A year ago', we say. 'It seems like another century.' But our forebears said: 'A century ago! It seems like yesterday'.

Here, then, is the storyteller's final responsibility: the reconciliation of tale and audience. Her tales are almost always rural and very seldom contemporary and yet the great majority of her audience live in city, town and suburb, and live at a time when social change has been so great that some characters, actions and attitudes within folk tales may seem unrecognizable, irrelevant or offensive.

The wise woman and the childe and the charcoal-burner: where are they now? The wicked stepmother and the impossibly virtuous third daughter: how can we cope with them? And the casual exhibitions of violence, all the routine beatings and imprisonments and chopping off of heads: are these useful models, especially when our audiences consist of children?

Each oral storyteller and writer interested not in rehashing but recreating and perpetuating traditional tales is bound to consider such difficult issues. But where an audience consists wholly or partly of children, she has further responsibilities, akin to those of parent and teacher.

Since the difference between adult and child is not one of intelligence, sensitivity or the imaginative faculty but, rather, of experience and the lack of it, this is plainly where a storyteller's responsibility lies.

It is not much use pretending to children that there are no horrors in the world, when they know perfectly well that there are. They know it from television and radio; they know it from the newspapers; and they know it from loose talk amongst adults. They know it every day.

So while it is natural to try to protect children from naked atrocities, it is likely to be counterproductive to suppress altogether the vein of cruelty in traditional tale. Have you come across this telling anecdote?

> There was a young boy whose pedagogically solemn parents resolved to do everything in their power to prevent their child from developing superstitious fears. They banned fairy tales from the household and saw to it that witches, giants, and other cannibalistic fiends were never once mentioned in the child's presence. All went according to plan until one night the parents awoke to the shrill cries of their son. Startled, they rushed to his bed only to learn that he was afraid of sleeping in the dark. They were even more startled after they asked the boy why he was afraid of sleeping in the dark, for the child's answer, punctuated by sobs, was: 'There's a complex hiding under my bed'.
>
> (Röhrich, 1976)

What is needed is for the storyteller, like the parent, to become the mediator or broker between children and the raw material of human experience. She must relay it but also interpret it. That is to say, the storyteller must consider and present her stories in an ethical light, in which good and bad behaviour have consequences both for the individual and society.

This said, I must admit I have come across perhaps half-a-dozen tales so irredeemably nasty and hopeless that it would be perverse (and perverted) to lay them before children, while there are others so sexually frank or deviant as to be completely inappropriate for the innocent eye and ear. I think, really, that a sensible working rule for the reteller for children is not to regard any subject as taboo, but not to confront children with behaviour or situations in which the only colour is unmitigated black despair.

These, then, are the five responsibilities shared by oral storyteller and writer. And I believe that careful consideration of them should lie at the heart of our re-enacting of traditional tale.

The staple diet of oral storyteller and writer alike is third person narrative: she said this, he saw that, they did the other. Or else, in the interests of immediacy: he says, she sees, they do.

But in reviewing the storyteller's responsibilities, I suggested that she must enter a tale and allow it to enter her. When this happens, the process of creation begins. And the cornerstone of remaking is the selection of the form which best enables the reteller to reveal the strength of her material and best supports the message or moral, however well hidden, that she wishes to convey.

This does not mean that the storyteller is duty-bound to invade and take over and recast each tale she uses. We all know of originals so well-judged and word-bright that we may do best to leave them more or less as they are, and play the role not of remaker but editor. I have sometimes found this to be the right course of action with the century-old versions by Joseph Jacobs.

In the same way, the storyteller may sometimes find her primary role is as translator. In retelling astounding tales such as 'Long Tom and the Dead Hand' and 'Samuel's Ghost' collected by Mrs Balfour during the 1980s, I have frankly done little more than come to grips with archaic Lincolnshire dialect and translate into modern English.

But let me describe three rather more radical strategies I have found fruitful when retelling traditional tales, which can be used by writer and storyteller alike.

One characteristic of our times has been the ubiquity of the outsider. I mean people driven from their homes by oppression, hunger or illness, herded into encampments which begin as temporary and end up as more or less permanent. I mean all those people who, by virtue of colour, culture or creed, find themselves alone or in very small minorities within the societies they live in. I mean the children of travellers in British primary and secondary schools. I mean the people in my own Norfolk village who were not born here but are, as I am, 'furriners'. I suppose I also mean, by extension, that part of each of us that believes she is a square peg in a round hole, and does not really quite fit in.

There are many traditional tales in which the separateness of the central character(s) is the very point of the tale. When A encounters X, Y and Z, what happens? Is there friction? Are they unable to rub along or do they come to accept they are all members of the same alphabet? The telling of tales revolving around conflict-resolution and tolerance and even delight in difference is valuable work. And because the central character is, at first anyhow, an isolated figure, there may be a case for reflecting this in the form of the retelling. How? Simply by telling the tale in the first person, from the viewpoint of the central character. At once, the reteller is working with 'I' and 'they'.

This device has two further advantages. It enables the 'I'-figure to reveal something of her thoughts and feelings without interrupting the rapid progression typical of traditional tale. And it enables the reteller directly to describe the familiar with new eyes.

The second of my three strategies takes its lead from the conviction of the medieval theologian, Duns Scotus, that each element of our planet, each stick and stone and granule of earth, has its own quiddity, if only we have time to dream our way into it; and from the recognition by Native Americans that each element has its own voice, if only we listen to it.

In considering how to retell the legend of church bells ringing underwater to warn sailors of danger – a tradition common to Dunwich in Suffolk and Mundesley in Norfolk and to Cardigan Bay and Lancashire and Brittany – I was guided by the fact that this is a tale in which many distinct and powerful forces are caught up in the conflict: cliff, church, village community, and the dead in the graveyard, are all at risk because of the fury of the night storm and destructive power of the sea.

So why not, I wondered, give a voice to each of these forces? Why not allow them to tell their own tale? As I drafted the tale 'Sea Tongue', I also hit upon a way of linking the end of each short section with the beginning of the next so as to sustain the narrative's momentum and imitate the tolling of a bell underwater:

> *(end)* I'll undermine the church and its graveyard. I'll chew on the bones of the dead.
> *(beginning)* We are the dead. We died in bed, we died on the sword. We fell out of the sky, we swallowed the ocean.

And again:

> *(end)* We live time out, long bundles of bone bedded in the cliff.
> *(beginning)* I am the cliff. Keep away from me. I'm jumpy and shrinking, unsure of myself. I may let you down badly.

(Crossley-Holland, 1997b).

Whether this form works or not, and whether it is imitable, is for others to say. But I offer it as one way in which form – effectively a fractured narrative – can underpin matter.

My third and last strategy is not so much a matter of form as context, and it arises from the responsibility of reteller, discussed earlier, to reconcile tale and audience.

What, in fact, are storyteller and writer to do when most of their material is rural (and ancient) when most of their audience is urban (and youthful)?

One answer is both simple and exacting: strip a tale down to its bare storyline, and then build it up again using modern characters and a modern setting. Sometimes this seems out of the question, because the storyline makes it so. In the case of some of Mrs Balfour's tales, for instance, the huge sucking fen, apparently so empty, in fact so full of threatening supernatural beings – boggarts and bogies and will-o'-the-wykes and squirming dead hands – appears to be so fundamental as to be irreplaceable.

But is this really so? I am thinking of sodden, eerie peat cuttings (such as those on the doorstep of Wilmslow in Cheshire) and of the concrete-and-wasteland of housing estates. There is actually no reason why a reteller should not plant stories such as 'The Dead Moon' and 'Yallery Brown' in such settings.

To do this kind of thing means, of course, that one is laying oneself open to the charge of making artificial transplants. But this would only be the case if the reteller were imaginatively deficient, and changed the setting without changing the cast. What I am suggesting is that writer or storyteller should effectively take an old story as a chassis on which to construct a new one. And this is, of course, precisely what has happened as traditional tales have travelled from generation to generation, country to country, and continent to continent. One storyteller removes the colour local to another, and redresses the bones of the tale with detail and colour familiar to her own audience.

I am not arguing that storytellers should always provide their youthful audiences with familiar settings, but that their settings should not always be unfamiliar. Otherwise, we accentuate the distance between retellings and children's experience, and that cannot be right.

Some storytellers may find the prospect of reinventing a tale in this manner rather daunting. I did, when I first tried it in my *British Folk Tales* with 'The Small-Tooth Dog' which begins in a sorry backstreet with a mugging (Crossley-Holland, 1987). But take heart! The process is less difficult and more fun than it may seem at first, and it is extremely valuable. At present, the stock of tales with urban or suburban and modern settings is small and largely American; we need to add to it.

Parents, teachers and librarians regularly introduce children to traditional tales, while British teachers, in accordance with the National Curriculum, also put them to work in the primary school classroom.

They ask children to predict the endings of tales half-told, to develop their ability to think logically; they use tales as quarries for language work and character study and as models for plot-building and descriptive writing; they lead discussions of tales so as to rehearse cause and effect, right and wrong, social consequences, religious beliefs, the existence of magic and the supernatural, the power of names and numbers. Teachers use traditional tales for hot-seating (in which a child pretends to be one of the characters in a tale, and answers questions from allcomers about her thoughts and feelings), and they use tales to point up the difference between thought and action. They use tales as springboards for geography and history projects, and they have children re-enact traditional tale in drama, music, dance and artwork.

All this activity is potentially extremely valuable, but it is also all secondary. In this chapter, I simply want to assert that none of it is or can be a substitute for a young child's primary experience of hearing or reading the tale itself. This is the moment at which a child may enter into deep communion, revelling in a tale's drama and music and patterning, apprehending without fully understanding that this story is also in some part her story, and unaware that she is animating the tradition by sharing in it.

It follows that teachers simply must root around for the best written versions they can find; and often, I know, this means they will be personally buying books for use in the classroom. It means they must do their utmost, as so many do, to become lively storytellers. And, though funds are invariably limited, it means they must try to bring writers and storytellers into direct contact with children in the classroom.

This is a lot to ask. But I do not think it is overstating the case to say that a child's experience of traditional tale is seminal. It can be a time of intensely experienced joy; it can lead to a lifelong love of story; and the quality of a child's involvement with the secondary activities described above is likely to be determined by it.

Research into the human brain indicates that brain activity is high when one is absorbing information through one sensory mode (hearing, for instance, or seeing) but low when one is using two sensory modes (hearing and seeing), as is the case when one watches and listens to television.

It follows that a child whose imagination is quickened by regularly listening to and reading tales will also be developing her ability to solve a mathematical problem or set up a science experiment. Indeed, I have heard teachers make the point that a child's hearing or reading of story has lasting implications for her whole learning capacity.

Of course there are some aspects of the oral tradition the writer cannot assimilate. She cannot raise or lower the voice, or speak in different tones, but only describe such differences:

> 'Somebody's been eating my porridge!' said the great, huge bear in his great, rough, gruff voice. 'Somebody's been eating my porridge!' said the middle bear in his middle voice. 'Somebody's been eating my porridge!' said the little, small, wee bear in his little, small, wee voice, 'and somebody has eaten it all up!'

Likewise, the writer cannot speed up or slow down a tale to anything like the same extent as an oral storyteller, and can only hint at the sound of silence.

In her valuable Signal Bookguide *Traditional Tales*, Mary Steele wrote that 'In printed form the traditional tale is really a script for the storyteller speaking, performing, acting a story'. (Steele, 1989) These words describe the circular nature of storytelling (water drawn up from the ocean must eventually return to the ocean!) and contain an implicit reminder to writers that since the first sources of traditional tale were always oral, they will be wise to imitate or find equivalents for such crucial elements of the oral tradition as immediacy and an air, however carefully calculated, of spur-of-the-moment improvisation.

But Mary Steele's words also indicate that writers are denied the use of expression or gesture, ranging from the raised forefinger or eyebrow to a kick of the foot or use of the whole body. The storyteller uses mouthfuls of air and a whole bag of oral-and-body tricks; the writer uses nothing but written words.

All a writer can offer, therefore, are the fruits of deliberation: well-considered shapeliness, so as to begin in expectation, achieve the right balance between a tale's basic structure and extraneous detail, and end in inevitability; and well-considered language, full of edge and colour and verve, so as to point up character, action and mood.

'Like – but oh how different! Different – but oh how like!' When we hear a tale well-told or read a story well-written, the work of some teller or writer with energy and wit and love of the human condition, we experience the same two responses. We know that by identifying, or half-identifying with a tale, we are coming close to ourselves and our fellow humans, and engaging in a kind of healing process. And we feel a delight in story that lasts, like a pervasive scent, long after we have forgotten the ins-and-outs of a particular tale.

So, in the end, this is what matters most: not this story, or that story, and not the primacy of the oral or the written tradition, but – once upon a time and ever after – the story's telling.

Remember, if you will, the wonderful exchange in Ronald Blythe's *Akenfield*: 'What was the song, Davie?' 'Never mind the song – it was the singing that counted.' (Blythe, 1969).

NOTE

This chapter is based on a talk given on 5 November 1997 at *It's the Words that Count: on the page and off the page*, a conference organized by the Society for Storytelling and Wandsworth Arts and Entertainments. It forms part of the Oracle Series published by the Society for Storytelling and is reprinted here with their kind permission.

REFERENCES

Blythe, R. (1969) *Akenfield*. London: Allen Lane.

Crossley-Holland, K. (1987) *British Folk Tales*. London: Orchard Books.

Crossley-Holland, K. (1997a) 'Diz' in the cycle 'Waterslain', in *Poems from East Anglia*. London: Enitharmon Press.

Crossley-Holland, K. (1997b) *The Old Stories*. Cambridge: Colt Books.

Dorson, R. (1968) *Peasant Customs and Savage Myths: Selections from the British Folklorists*. London: Routledge and Kegan Paul.

O'Sullivan, S. (1996) *Folktales of Ireland*. London: Routledge and Kegan Paul.

Röhrich, L. (1976) 'Sage und Märchen: Erzahlforschung heute', trans. Tatar, M. (1987), in *The Hard Facts of the Grimms' Fairy Tales*. Princeton: Princeton University Press.

Simpson, J. (1980) *British Dragons*. London: B.T. Batsford.

Steele, M. (1989) *Traditional Tales*. Stroud: Thimble Press.

Zipes, J. (1996) *Revisiting the Storyteller*. London: Daylight Press for the Society for Storytelling, Oracle Series No.1.

Chapter 2

Betsy Whyte and the Dreaming

Hugh Lupton

THE MAN WITHOUT A STORY

There once lived a man and his name was Jimmy.

He was one of those people who have nothing to say for themselves.

If he sat down with you at the table for a meal he would only move his chin to chew his food. He had nothing to say at all.

Now, Jimmy worked for a farmer, a wealthy and a generous man with many hundreds of acres, but a man with a reputation as a dabbler in the black arts – in dark magic.

Every autumn, when the harvests had been brought in, when the stooks had been stacked and the sacks were bulging with grain, when the apples had been racked and the bushel bags had been loaded into the lofts of the barns . . . when all the work had been done, this farmer would have a big harvest-home supper. All the workers on the farm and their families would be invited. They would sit down at long trestle tables in the great tithe barn. There would be bottles of brandy and whiskey, there would be barrels of beer, and outside in the farmyard there would be beds of glowing charcoal with whole roast sheep turning on spits and dropping their fat into the flames.

Throughout the feast the farmer would sit at a high table at one end of the barn, presiding over the proceedings.

It was a tremendous meal, the high point of the year.

And each year, when the feast was finished, the farmer would get up to his feet and hit the table with his fist.

'My friends', he would say, 'the feast is over and the time has come for the ceilidh to begin. As you all know, the rules are very simple and they go like this: tell a story, sing a song, show your bum or out you're gone!'

And each year the farmer would set two cups on the table-top: a golden cup for the best story of the night and a silver cup for the biggest lie of the night.

'Now, who's to begin?'

And everybody would have to do something, and if there was anyone who had nothing to tell or to sing, then he or she would have to pay a forfeit.

And so it was on the particular night of my story, the telling and the singing began. One person followed another and the farmer sat and listened, sometimes laughing, sometimes wiping a tear from the corner of his eye. Hour followed hour in what seemed like no time at all. The bottles and the barrels began to grow empty and still the stories and songs continued.

Now, all evening Jimmy had been sitting among the shadows at the back of the barn trying not to catch the farmer's eye. Hour followed hour in what seemed to him an eternity. Outside the moon rose and set, the sky brightened with stars.

It was approaching the early hours of morning when the farmer saw him.

'Jimmy! We've had nothing from you yet tonight. Come on man, let's have a song or a story!'

Jimmy got up to his feet. Every song he'd ever heard seemed to have disappeared from his mind, every story had vanished. Behind his forehead there was a terrible blank. He looked at the farmer and said nothing.

The farmer shook his head:

'Jimmy, you've neither a tune nor a tale, so you'll have to pay a forfeit. What I want you to do is this, go out of the barn and down the hill to the edge of the lake. You'll see on the shingle there's a little boat full of water. Bale the water out of it then come back up to the barn.'

Jimmy nodded, and with every eye watching him he shuffled out of the barn. He made his way down the hill, and sure enough, by the light of the stars, he could see there was a boat on the shingle. He crouched down and peered into it. There was a little tin cup floating on the water inside. He picked it up and began to bale. He baled and he baled until there was only some muddy water left sloshing on the bilge-boards at the bottom of the boat.

He climbed inside and was just scraping the last of the water over the edge when, all of a sudden of its own accord, the little boat shot out across the water. It shot out with such sudden force that Jimmy fell over backwards, cracked his head against the back of the boat and fell unconscious onto the bilge-boards.

The next thing he knew was that the little boat was rocking from side to side. He sat up, rubbed his head and looked about himself.

In every direction the water stretched into darkness. Jimmy thought to himself:

'Well, there's only one thing for it, I'll have a smoke on my pipe and wait for the sun to rise.'

He reached across to pull his pipe from his waist-coat pocket ... but his waist-coat had disappeared and where it should have been there was a soft cotton blouse. And where the pocket of the waist-coat should have been there was a lump growing where there had never been a lump before. Soft, it was, against the palm of his hand. He reached across to the other side and there was another, just like the first. He reached down with his hands and felt his hips – they were wider than he remembered. And where his trousers should have been there was a skirt. There were stockings on his legs, and where his old tackety boots had once been, there were little leather slippers!

Jimmy looked about himself and he saw, on the bench of the boat, there was a handbag. He picked it up and put it onto what had once been his knee and was now his lap. He opened it and rummaged inside. There was a mirror. He peered into it. By the light of the stars he saw the reflection of his face ... and it wasn't his face! There was long hair falling down over the shoulders, the lips were full and red. He dropped the mirror into the handbag. He grabbed the oars that were lying in the bottom of the boat, fitted them into the rowlocks and began to row.

He rowed and he rowed, this way and that way over the water, until, at last, he saw the first light of morning rising over the hills.

Jimmy pulled towards the edge of the lake.

Soon the prow scraped against the shingle.

Jimmy lifted her skirts and climbed out of the boat. She looked about herself; this was a place she'd never seen before. There was a path running along the lake-shore. She started walking.

A thin, chill drizzle began to sleek down out of the sky. Jimmy shivered and held herself against the cold.

As she was walking she saw, striding towards her through the rain, there was a young man.

As soon as he caught sight of Jimmy he stopped and doffed his cap and smiled.

'Hello', he said.

'Hello', said Jimmy, her voice had changed.

'I've never seen you around here before. What's your name?'

'Jimmy', said Jimmy.

'Jimmy, that's a strange name for a young woman. Where do you come from?'

Poor Jimmy, she wasn't much good at stories. All she could say was:

'I don't know. I don't really know.'

'Well listen, my old grandmother lives half a mile along the road, why don't you come and warm yourself up in front of her fire and we'll make a pot of tea?'

'All right', said Jimmy.

And so she followed the young man along the path to the old woman's cottage. She was welcomed inside. She was shown a place by the fire and she stood warming herself, the steam rising from her wet clothes.

The old woman brought her a cup of tea.

'Where do you come from, my dear?'

Jimmy sipped the tea.

'I don't know. I don't really know.'

The old woman whispered to her grandson:

'She must have lost her memory, she'd better stay here with us for a while.'

And so it was that Jimmy stayed in the little cottage with the old woman and the young man. The days passed and the weeks passed. Whenever they asked her where she was from, the same answer came:

'I don't know. I don't really know.'

The weeks passed and the months passed, and Jimmy helped the old woman with the milking and the baking and the jobs about the house.

And as for the young man, he became more and more interested in Jimmy. They began walking out together over the hills above the lake.

Sometimes Jimmy would look across to the far side . . . but it was a long way and nothing was clear, she began to forget about her old life.

One day, when they were out walking, they sat down on some soft heather on the brow of a hill. The young man turned to Jimmy:

'Jimmy, I'll tell you what, we could get married, you and me.'

Jimmy looked across at him. She thought to herself: 'Here I am and this is me and . . . well, why not.' She smiled.

'All right', she said, 'all right then, let's get married.'

And so there was a wedding.

And a year later a wonderful thing happened. Jimmy gave birth to a fine baby boy.

And the years and the years passed, two more sons were born and Jimmy was happy. She was happy living with her husband and the three boys. She'd never been so happy in all her life.

And ten years passed.

Then, one day, they went for a walk. All five of them went for a walk together along the path that ran beside the shore-line of the lake.

Suddenly Jimmy stopped in her tracks.

There on the shingle beside the lake was the little boat, just as it had been all those years before. She turned to her husband and her three sons.

'You sit down beneath that tree a moment, I must go and have a look at that little boat.'

They sat down in the shade of the tree and Jimmy went across the shingle. She looked at the boat. She peered inside. There, lying on the bilge-boards, was the tin baler. She was amazed. She lifted up her skirts and climbed into the boat. She sat down and picked up the baler.

She was just passing it from hand to hand, thinking about the time she'd crossed the water all those years before, when all of a sudden the little boat shot out across the water of its own accord. It shot out with such sudden force that Jimmy fell over backwards and cracked her head against the back of the boat. She fell unconscious onto the bilge-boards.

The next thing she knew was that the boat was rocking from side to side. She opened her eyes and the sky above her was bright with stars.

She looked about herself, in every direction the water stretched into darkness.

She shouted across the water:

'My husband! My boys!' Her voice had changed, and there was no answer.

She rubbed her head where she'd cracked it against the boat. Her long hair was gone. She touched her face; there were bristles growing on her cheek and chin. She looked down. Where her blouse should have been, there was an old waist-coat with a pipe-stem sticking out of the pocket.

She was wearing muddy trousers and on her feet there were a pair of tackety boots.

She shouted again:

'My husband! My boys!'

There was silence.

Then she saw the first light of morning rising over the hills.

Jimmy lifted the oars into the rowlocks and pulled for the edge of the lake. Soon the prow was scraping against the shingle.

He climbed out of the boat. He saw at the top of the hill there were lights shining. He made his way towards them.

He saw the lights were coming from a great barn.

He crossed the yard and pushed open the doors. The barn was full of people. He ran inside.

'My husband, my boys, where are they, where are they?'

And then he saw the farmer, sitting at the high table at the far end of the barn. The farmer looked at him and smiled.

'What are you talking about Jimmy?'

'I was married! I had three sons! Where are they?'

The farmer shook his head.

'Jimmy, you've only been gone ten minutes, you'd better tell us the whole story!'

So Jimmy made his way across the barn floor and stood before the farmer. He told the whole story from beginning to end. He poured out his heart. When he'd finished the farmer said:

'Jimmy, not only was that the best story we've had all night, it was also the biggest lie. You'd better take the both of these.'

And he gave Jimmy the silver and the golden cup.

And from that day onwards Jimmy always had a story to tell.

Whenever tales were being told, it would be: 'Jimmy, tell us the one about the time you crossed over the water and gave birth to all those children!' And Jimmy would tell his story.

But sometimes when he was lying in bed, about to fall asleep, he would think about his husband and his three sons, and he would wonder just where they were, and just what had happened to them.

And that is the end of my story: if it be bitter or if it be sweet, carry some away and bring some back!

A CHAIN OF VOICES

There is a tradition among the travellers that when you tell a story, the person you heard it from is standing behind you. Standing behind me as I told that story was Betsy Whyte. You might not have been able to see her, but she was there, an old woman, modest in cardigan and blouse, standing very straight and still like a little girl at school reciting something in Assembly. Her voice, a lilting Scottish voice, a thin old woman's voice with a twist of laughter at the back of it, a voice roughened by a lifetime's smoking. Betsy died ten years ago, but there is no mistaking her presence behind me as I tell the story. And who was standing behind her as she told the story? Who knows! One of the Townsleys probably, the big, scattered traveller family she grew up in. Perhaps a great uncle, whittling a stick into the flames of the fire, in a woollen vest and old corduroys, looking just as he was some summer night in the nineteen-twenties. And who stood behind him ... and behind him ... and behind her?

Whenever I tell a traditional story I am part of a process, a new link in a chain of voices. Behind me are all the people who have carried the story before me. As I tell the story they are speaking through me. I am a medium, I am part of a game of Chinese whispers that has been going on for hundreds of years. Even if the storyteller is taking the tale from a book, he or she can be sure that the printed word represents only a small part of the story's life. It has been carried on the tongue before and it is being returned to its proper medium. As Alan Garner has written, the life of the traditional stories is 'in the music; it is in the language: not phonetics, grammar and syntax, but pitch and cadence and the colour of the word' (Garner, 1984).

So what is this thing that is being passed through time, that I receive from Betsy Whyte (or whoever) and pass on to you? I have been calling it 'story' but it might just as easily be nursery rhyme, ballad, joke, urban legend, riddle or myth. It could be anything from Humpty Dumpty to Beowulf to the book of Genesis. What is it? It is the material that appears in the anthologies as having been 'written' by Anon, or Anonymous. It is, in fact, the creation of the ancestors, the nameless ones, the people without name or number who have told it, shaped it, sung it, adapted, adopted, translated, transcribed, remembered and re-membered it. It might have no more purpose than to get a child to go to sleep, or to elicit a sudden chill shudder, or it might contain profound religious truth. It might even do all three!

The point is that this material is not the creation of any one person; it is universal, it is everyone's creation and everyone's property. It carries in it something of everyone who has told it or sung it before us (whether it is a word, or an inflection, or a moment of musical ornamentation, or a turn of phrase) like the dark shine on a medieval church pew-end, polished by six hundred years of handling. It is a shared cultural invention.

This body of material that our collective imagination, working over thousands of years, has precipitated, these images, histories, melodies, rhymes and tales, along with the dialects and languages that carry them, along with the landscapes they refer to, are what the Australian Aborigines would refer to as our 'Dreaming'. They are at the root of our cultural identity. If a nation or a tribe has a soul, then this Dreaming, this dreamstuff, is it. And in our culture we are forgetting it.

For two hundred years, since the Industrial Revolution, we have been busily forgetting it and a large proportion of it has gone. What does it mean for a culture to have forgotten its dreaming, to have ignored its stories, forgotten its songs, mocked its dialects, debased and suppressed its languages and desecrated its landscapes (and all these things are connected)?

I was very fortunate to meet Betsy Whyte. There are few people left in Britain who carry the old stories from an unbroken oral tradition. It was because her family had always lived on the edge of society, because her schooling was an occasional and haphazard affair that she managed to dodge the dominant world-view that would have inevitably caused her to devalue and underestimate the wealth she carried. For me she stands as a representative of that intimate, hidden, human, inner resource that can really only be communicated from one person to another, and which stands at odds with all the prevailing machinery and morality of our time. She is the polar opposite of the morality that Ted Hughes has called 'the morality of the camera':

A morality utterly devoid of any awareness of the requirement of the inner world.

(Hughes, 1994)

It is a morality that looks at the Dreaming and sees nothing, that looks over my shoulder and sees no-one.

Betsy, in my personal mythology, represents the Dreaming. And in telling a story as she would have done we are doing something radical. A story given in quiet, away from all distraction (allowing the subtle activity of pictures in the mind, allowing the music of the spoken word, allowing the merging of inner and outer worlds, allowing a real, human interaction) is a radical act. Although it is quite outside the expectations of our society, and for many people – both children and adults – quite outside their ordinary experience, people are thirsty for it.

In a traditional or pre-literate society, the lore, the Dreaming is passed from parent or grandparent to family, from master to apprentice, from priest to novice, in talk from one person to another. There is a knower, someone who carries the knowledge, and there are those who receive it. Very often in these cultures and societies it has been the elderly who have been the carriers and disseminators of traditional knowledge (just as

Betsy carried it and passed it on to me). But what happens now? To quote Alan Garner again:

> In society now the old are no longer a source of learning and no-one listens to what they could say. Defensively they have stopped talking, and they make a virtue of dying with their knowledge unshared. Nothing comparable is replacing that knowledge, and the young inherit nothing of their own . . . . A healthy future grows from its past; but today the links are being broken, both in the particular and the general culture. The loss of traditional fairy tales . . . is just such a debility.
>
> (Garner, 1984)

As educators, whether parents or teachers, we should be aware of our place in the journey from past into future. We have taken on the role of passing knowledge to the next generation. If anyone is in a position to give the Dreaming to its rightful inheritors, it is us. In a traditional culture the children are listening to and absorbing stories all the time. Although there may be layers of meaning that will not be revealed to them until years later, they move with ease and delight in the vivid world of story, storying and remembering. As adults we are in a position to give the stories to the children, and there need be no aim or objective beyond being a sort of middle-man (or woman) between past and future. In Armenia the storytellers end a performance by saying: 'Three golden apples fell from the sky: one for you who listened; one for I who told; and one for those who first found this story many years ago'. As educators we should be entitled to the second apple. This means making books available, of course, but primarily it means reading and telling the stories aloud.

What is happening when this process of telling a story takes place? The function of the storyteller has always been to straddle two worlds. One foot is in the place where the story is being told, holding the attention of the listeners; the other foot is in the place where the story happens. To the Australian Aborigines everything that is not imme-diately visible has gone into the Dreaming. A storyteller, therefore, has one foot in the here-and-now and one foot in the Dreaming, and he (or she) mediates between the two. He might be telling a joke, a historical narrative, a fairy tale, a true story from his own past . . . the process is always the same. His outer eye looks towards his audience, his inner eye searches out the story, and the words on his tongue relay the inner world to the outer.

Betsy Whyte's story about Jimmy's journey across the water has always seemed to me to be a metaphor for the journey a storyteller makes with his audience. What takes ten years to happen in one world takes ten minutes in another. That is the way stories work: ten years, a lifetime, the creation of the world can be told in twenty minutes. And Jimmy, telling his story after his return across the water, has been to that other world, he has seen it, he has entered the landscape, he has known the pain – of course he wins the gold and silver cups! The more a storyteller enters the Dreaming the better he'll be at it. But it is not a journey to make lightly, and there are responsibilities involved.

So, at the present time there is a thirst for the stories, a need for them (even among those who do not know how thirsty and needy they are). There are more and more people interested in syphoning the Dreaming, sinking new wells into it and slaking this shared thirst. Over the last fifteen years there has been an extraordinary revival of interest in traditional storytelling. The trouble is that after two hundred years of indifference and neglect, our own dreaming has become rather bookish and thin. Neil Philip, in his controversial introduction to his collection of English folk tales, has written: 'Of all the major folk literatures, that of England is probably the scantiest.' (Philip, 1992) It begins to get richer when we cross the borders into Scotland and Wales (and even richer still beyond the Irish Sea) but even there the Betsy Whytes are few and far between. How do we find out what a living oral tradition might have been?

Fortunately we do not have to go far. The Indian and Caribbean/African communities (along with other ethnic minorities) have always been in close contact with their oral cultures. If there was a tendency for the first immigrant generation to try to adapt to the 'English way', the second generation, born in Britain and growing up as British citizens, have instinctively recognized the need for this dream-stuff. They have celebrated their own cultural wealth and it has fed a tremendous charge into the artistic climate of this country – not least among storytellers. Like many others, admiring the vitality of these cultures, I was led to ask the question: 'What have we got that compares with this?' This took me back to the stories that I had always known underlay our culture: the Greek myths, the Bible, Joseph Jacobs' fairy tales, Robin Hood, the Child ballads, the Norse myths, the Arthurian tales, the Mabinogion, the Ulster Cycle, the rich fragments in Katherine Briggs' monumental *Dictionary of British Folk-tales*. But now I was approaching them with the possibility of the exuberance of live performance echoing in my ears and imagination. The living rhythms of pulse and breath began to replace the old bookishness. The 'British Dreaming' was beginning to come to life in my imagination.

All this talk of 'national dreaming' might set alarm bells ringing. A blinkered nationalism can contain the seeds of racial intolerance – and we only have to look to the former Yugoslavia to see how the heroic epic tales of the Serbs have been used to validate 'ethnic cleansing'. It is a difficult issue. A traditional heritage is a collective soul. Without it we may find ourselves profoundly at sea, but at the same time, a nationalistic 'Britishness' or 'Englishness' could be a dangerous thing.

It is my belief that the stories offer a way out of this dilemma. The more deeply we go into them, the more we discover the same themes, images and motifs appearing in tales from all over the world. P. L. Travers has written:

> ... the self-same themes seem to emerge, as though something in the psyche of a race had ripened and produced a fruit that corresponded, not in its form but in its substance, with the fruit of all other races. The fact that the same stories arise in India, the Middle East, Europe, the Americas, as well as China and Japan is an intimation that their proper soil and seeding place is not in any geographical location, but in man himself.
>
> (Travers, 1989)

The implications of this are tremendous. The more deeply we go into our 'National Dreaming' the more it turns out to be an 'International Dreaming'. The stories, on the one hand, celebrate local difference and regional or national identity; on the other hand they celebrate the universal humanity of all peoples. P. L. Travers goes on to say: 'This alone could ensure, if we believed it (I'm speaking mythologically, of course) that no-one on the planet need be a stranger to any other.' Betsy Whyte did not know it, but the story she told has equivalents in many different traditions, most markedly in one of the tales from the ancient Sanskrit cycle of stories entitled 'The King and the Corpse'.

Maybe if we looked hard enough at the ghosts behind the ghosts behind Betsy's shoulder, they would lead us back to an Indian original. I think it is more likely that, by virtue of our shared humanity, the same themes and dreams emerge spontaneously, 'as alike as the lines on the palm of the human hand' (Hughes, 1994).

REFERENCES

Garner, A. (1984) *Book of British Fairy Tales*. London: Collins.

Hughes, T. (1994) 'Myth and Education', in *Winter Pollen*. London: Faber.

Philip, N. (1992) *The Penguin Book of English Folktales*. London: Penguin.

Travers, P. L. (1989) 'The World of the Hero', in *What the Bee Knows*. Wellingborough: Aquarian Press.

Chapter 3

Developing Teaching as Storytelling

Grant Bage

Does the ancient art of storytelling have a place in future classrooms? This chapter will answer that question by speaking from experience of an ongoing research and development project promoting storytelling in education. In some homage to Egan (1989) the initiative is called TASTE, teaching-as-storytelling. Like Egan the project argues that oral (and then) literary storytelling remain deeply significant for teaching and learning, sometimes in contrast to the shallowness and ambivalence with which educational policy-makers treat 'story'.

One reason for story's perennial significance is that children still seem to adore it. In a multimedia world young consumers eagerly exchange leisure time and hard cash for old stories repackaged and new stories made via cartoon, film, TV, video, computer game, CD ROM and website (e.g. Hilton, 1996; Robinson, 1997). Stories in older guise also continue to underpin the teaching of literacy in modern English schools. The first National Curriculum in English (DES, 1989) and the National Literacy Strategy (DfEE, 1997, 1998) enshrined written and spoken narratives on the state's curricular high altar. The Labour government's successful 1997 election campaign led so strongly with 'education, education and education' that David Blunkett, the Education Secretary, pledged his future on improving literacy as measured by national English tests for 11-year-olds. A cartoon graphically illustrates his promise. In a classroom David Blunkett points to writing on the blackboard and asks the seated class to repeat 'My job depends on your literacy and numeracy – Altogether now, one hundred times'. The punchline was that none of them could (*Times Educational Supplement*, 12 March 1999). England's educational life in the new millennium rests upon public and political assumptions about the entwined educational value of stories and literacy: but to what extent should these remain unchallenged, or might they need reinventing, for a new age?

One such assumption concerns the craving of governments to produce tangible improvements in educational 'standards'. This results in pressures upon teachers to concentrate upon learning measurable by standardized means such as tests, tables and targets. Such pressures heighten with every hour that education occupies the political centre-stage and have resulted, amongst many other things, in a National Literacy Framework (DfEE, 1998). Although this draws from a rich range of storied texts, detailed empirical and theoretical studies have long shown that stories help children acquire far more than a narrow range of literacy skills. Stories give children knowledge about the world and about living in it: stories develop humanity and personality.

> A child's fairy tale, for example, does not simply teach that the world is full of witches and giants. In another sense the tale uses fantasy characters ... to give body and form to the child's worst shapeless fears – and in the process to begin to conquer them ... Literature is one of the many instruments of socialization which a culture provides.
>
> (Applebee, 1978; see also Wells, 1986; Meek *et al.*, 1977)

Centralized curricula such as the National Literacy Framework and their associated commercial spin-offs focus upon describing and teaching language as detailed steps through a hierarchical scheme of knowledge and skills. Unless carefully handled by teachers such curricula risk marginalizing or fragmenting children's learning from the wider values of story referred to above by Applebee.

A second and linked assumption concerns the 'moral' or 'meanings' of stories. Narratives have to end, and endings necessitate judgements by the teller (White, 1987). Any teacher who has made children wait for a story's ending will also testify that endings matter to listeners, often desperately. The end of a powerful story, though, is not simply its final word. Nor is it just a discrete teaching objective, such as whether the story has helped seven- and eight-year-old children to 'identify and discuss main and recurring characters, evaluate their behaviour and justify views' (DfEE, 1998). Further and perhaps higher ends exist. Did the story leave children wanting to hear or read another one? What did the story say to them, and were the tellers and listeners sufficiently motivated by the story to think about and decide what it 'meant'?

The knowledge stories embody, and the moral meanings they offer should therefore be considered as of first and not second order educational importance. Teaching strategies valuing preset objectives, or the isolated development of skills over such qualities, can sideline some of the most valuable things that stories actually do for learners: motivate them to think about and use language for intrinsic means, not extrinsic schemes.

Neither of these two attributes of story, expanding knowledge about the world and increasing awareness of values, are easily quantifiable within current systems of educational accountancy. Nor do they sit comfortably within the confines of literacy hours or national schemes, the 'hurry along curricula' that have dominated English education since 1988 (Dadds, 1998). Yet knowledge and values have always been so fundamental to stories that Aristotle could urge over 2000 years ago that, for moral reasons 'the officials known as inspectors of children's welfare ought to pay attention to deciding what kind of literature and stories children [under five] are to hear' (trans. Sinclair, 1962).

Modern, government-led desires to measure literacy learning in numbers, and the ancient desire to moralize through it, push contemporary storytelling teachers into an awkward corner. The curriculum is now so crowded that to justify significant storytelling on the grounds of simple pleasure is increasingly difficult, especially where schools feel pressurized by low literacy scores and ambitious year-on-year improvement targets. Similarly, valuing the morals and knowledge to be had from stories, even the notion of developing common values and cultures, can seem a gargantuan task for teachers in a world where commercial pressures, social change and cultural diversity may be perceived as splintering consensus and straining community.

Need this be so? 'TASTE', or teaching-as-storytelling, is a research and development project which comes at the perceived problems of say poor literacy, dull teaching or educational apathy from another, almost opposite direction. Inspired by practical and personal experiences of teaching (e.g. Bage, 1995, 1999, Collins, 1999) and the example of others (e.g. Egan, 1989), this project tries to use stories to improve education without standardizing either. It does so in three ways. Firstly, it values the oral tradition, and speaking and listening, as highly as the literary tradition, and reading and writing. Secondly, professional storytellers are taken into classrooms for sustained periods. Their example encourages teachers, children, parents and the community to tell and listen to as many stories as they can, from as many different genres as they can, for as wide a range of curriculum subjects as possible. Thirdly, and in conjunction with the previous two aims, it involves researching and telling stories to help define a locality and its people, yet connects them with the wider world. These aims have been pursued with schools in two areas represented elsewhere in this book: in King's Lynn with the lead storyteller being Hugh Lupton (see chapter 2); and in Greenwich, with the lead storyteller being Fiona Collins (see chapter 4). Both areas and the 13 schools involved face many challenges, particularly a wide range of socio-economic deprivation and often poor previous achievements in literacy and other standardized tests of educational attainment.

Such a project not only swims against current nationalizing and standardizing educational tides; it also has to contend with older traditions tending to the same, if for different reasons. The editor's introduction to an Edwardian collection of stories about English History illustrates some of the typical difficulties this tradition presents:

> A little over a thousand years ago Alfred the Great was King ... only of part of England. Today the King of England rules over the greatest Empire that the world has even seen. The British people have overrun the earth and by their strength of character have made history wherever they have set foot ...   Remember and consider the glories of this country, and how every child can help to keep it great and glorious by leading a true and straightforward life, by being obedient to those in authority over them, and by honouring their present king ...
>
> (Vredenburg, n.d.)

Such stories would be unusable in English schools of the third millennium. Their style is outdated and their content embodies values of a prior, imperialist and even racist age. Does this mean that an initiative such as TASTE must discard the tradition of educational storytelling from which such writing emanates? Perhaps not, for the literary and historical picture introduced by Captain Vredenburg was more complex than first sight suggests. The imperialist and anglo-centric tradition his thought represented was, within the covers of the same book, challenged by one of its authors: Edith Nesbit.

Edith Nesbit was a Fabian socialist and an inhabitant of Eltham, south–east London, the district in which the TASTE project has been working a century later. A TASTE teacher has named her class in Nesbit's memory; another teaches in the same building where Nesbit provided Christmas parties for the children of the local poor; and stories about Nesbit's life have been developed by the TASTE team. Nesbit was a radical thinker who refuted conservative assumptions about English historical story-telling. Instead, she used story to challenge the wealthy and powerful, as in this instance:

> All the rebellions in Edward the Sixth's time were not about the Prayer Book ... for the people of England were, as usual, being oppressed and ill-treated by the rich ... The rich lords ... used to enclose a field or a wood here and there with a fence, and then say it was their own, and that the common people had no right to it. There was a great rebellion against this theft – for it was nothing less – and it would have been well for the poor of England if that rebellion had been successful.
>
> (Nesbit, n.d.)

Can modern teachers and storytellers similarly remake contemporary educational storytelling to improve teaching and learning, challenge established interests and embody diversity? The TASTE project exists to experiment with such goals. The remainder of this chapter therefore draws from interviews with five TASTE teachers to illustrate some outcomes they have witnessed from participating in TASTE. Two are from a 3–11 Nursery and Primary school in Greenwich (Shirley and Jo), where they worked with Fiona Collins (see chapter 4). The other three are from two schools in King's Lynn: Louise (Nursery and Infant School) and Kae and Maggi (a 3–11 Nursery and Primary school), who worked with Hugh Lupton (see chapter 2). For the purposes of this discussion, these teachers' comments have been analysed and ordered under preliminary headings.

STARTING WITH STORYTELLING: TEACHERS AND CHILDREN

Only one of the teachers in this account (Shirley) had considerable experience of story in her initial training; in fact she has since pursued storytelling as a hobby. Shirley's Year 6 colleague Jo, in her second year of teaching in Greenwich, had always 'sort of prided myself on the way which I read a story, and brought a story to life' but 'had never ... told'. When she went on the first TASTE project course she thought 'Oh no, I can't do that in front of my children ... But they thought it was brilliant and so we have learnt together ... ' From King's Lynn Louise, a Year 1/2 teacher, similarly describes how through her involvement with TASTE:

> Something struck me. When I am ... taking assemblies or groups of other children ... you don't need the book. You will tell a much better story, even if it has come from a book, if you read it first, think it through, and you tell the story as opposed to reading it.

Kae had used story and drama in her previous teaching experience. She also describes learning, through TASTE project involvement, how more formalized open-ings and endings to a story added to its educational value.

> I think just coming in and saying 'here is a story I am going to start now' is no way to do it. You have got to explain something about the story setting, something about what you

are going to do . . . A good start, a clean ending so they know where things are. There are rules to follow and that is important for colleagues as well as children.

Children were similarly motivated through story. Kae describes how making, performing and writing stories with her and her colleague Maggi's Year 3/4 children improved the self-image of the class:

> Quite often they are the children that don't get chosen to do things, because they have difficulties with language, so they are very proud of themselves. One of my little girls, after she had done the performance, she read it out, she took her story for her mother to see. I haven't been able to get it back yet because she was so proud of herself . . . She has taken a pride in her work which before was not there.

From another angle Shirley describes how storytelling helped her to establish classroom relationships and order:

> I have always told masses of stories . . . because I have found that when you have got a whole group of children sitting on a carpet, particularly ones that you don't know, if you tell and have got eye contact, they are just drawn into the story . . . If you have no book . . . the children and you develop a relationship much, much quicker. I always tell a lot of stories when I get a new class and it works.

Kae expresses similar sentiments: 'Simply telling stories is a nice social activity. If our children didn't enjoy them so much they wouldn't sit there and soak them up the way they do.'

TURNING EXPERIENCE INTO THOUGHT: CHILDREN USING STORY

Earlier in this chapter I claimed that storytelling and listening prompt not just the development of literacy, but also the thinking that underlies literacy. Kae argues likewise, 'I don't see how anybody can cope with their life and their language if they haven't got a wealth of stories in their head to draw on'. Her fellow Year 3/4 teacher Maggi testifies how through engagement with stories her children's thinking developed alongside their language:

> They are holding several layers of story or plot, several ideas in their mind. The accuracy of their recall is very, very strong and their questioning skills have improved too. When they first worked with Hugh they would ask very obvious questions and ask the same question two or three times . . . By the time they had worked with him for a couple of sessions the questioning was much more focused, they were listening to each other's answers and taking the questions to a much deeper level.

For Shirley, this is a defining educational characteristic of traditional stories:

> Most traditional stories are actually on themes that are . . . meant to teach. It is step families, it is people who are lost, it is conflicts and that kind of thing. Traditional stories

tend to be traditional because they still carry meaning and the children seem to pick up on that. So they are actually stories about things they want to hear about ... it may be a princess but she is actually in a very real situation and it is something that they can relate to ...

New language and new plots forged new ways of thinking and seeing the world. Maggi describes how:

Imagery that came into play [through storytelling] was something that the children would not have encountered. The very simple idea of taking an every day object and imagining it as an animal is well outside their scope of experience ... made them look at the language they do have in a totally different way.

Kae agrees. The typically restricted nature of her children's everyday language in school contrasted vividly with:

The way the Anglo Saxon stories were told by Hugh. No, we wouldn't have come across rhythms of language like that ... the use of some of the words and the descriptions of some of the characters.

COMMUNICATING THOUGHT THROUGH LANGUAGE: CHILDREN USING STORY

Purposeful, varied and rich speaking and listening has been a prerequisite and an outcome of this project. Jo, in her first year of using storytelling as a teacher, described how the Reception class and Year 1 had told stories and taken assembly. Meanwhile her Year 6 children:

... really gelled as a class because they have had this common thread where they were all learning stories together ... we had a storytelling fair ... one of the children in my class ... had just come over from Somalia. She was so quiet but you could just hear this voice booming through the whole room and it was her. And she thought 'Gosh, I can do this, I have got stories from my country that I could tell and people would love them'. It was great and she has come right out of her shell.

Her colleague Shirley sketches similar benefits across the primary age range. Stories gave a structure and a reason to talk, which in turn lent momentum to reading and writing:

In this particular area a lot of the children come in language impoverished and they really haven't got the oral skills. Without the oral skills they actually can't transfer anything to paper, because ... they have got something to say but they can't express themselves that well. Somehow the stories have been a way through that with a lot of them ...

Working with stories modelled richer language use for children. Maggi describes Year 3/4 children in King's Lynn:

> Definitely putting in more detail in their spoken language ... description is coming through and they are beginning to understand that their audience needs a few more details before they can fully understand.

Her colleague Kae agrees:

> One thing my group has done a lot more is that they have moved from telling a story to actually using their hands and some gesture to help enhance the story. So instead of just saying 'He was big' they have at least moved on to 'He was gigantic and enormous' which is a great leap forward for a speaker. So they are embellishing their stories, which I was very pleased about.

Such learning comes from listening:

> Part of the project for our children has been ... the quality of their listening has improved tremendously. Because the stories were not easy, they were quite complicated, with complicated plots and difficult names and they had to listen very carefully. We have found that they are listening much more carefully, hearing things and being able to listen for longer. That has been a very important thing for us because listening is a skill that some of our children are not particularly good at, so that has been a major plus.

Unprompted and from the other side of town, Louise observed a similar phenomenon with Year 1 and Year 2 children. She outlines how the regular use of oral stories over a year helped to develop structure, ideas and the children's own use of spoken and then written descriptive language:

> They have thought more about how to take one idea and to build it and make it grow, and also talking to someone and getting over what you have experienced. How do you get that over to somebody else? How do you engage their attention? It is going to help with their writing, it is going to help with their speaking and listening as well. They have learnt that there is so much more than just what happens, there is so much more on the descriptive side that they could be putting into their own stories ... that this embellishment really engages someone's attention ... Their ideas and the stories have become more detailed.

Children's reading and writing also appeared to benefit from TASTE, as shown by English SATs results from Shirley and Jo's Year 6 classes in Greenwich:

> We got good SATs results ... a lot better on the reading than on the writing. When I analysed what had happened in my class the children at the top end had done OK, but the children at the bottom had done incredibly well ... I think a lot of that ... is because they had finished, they had a whole story and they had stories that they could draw on ... It is multi-layered – there is everything about the story. The effect it has on their writing, it makes them interested in story and it makes them want to read.

> (Shirley)

In conjunction the teachers also used the technique of 'storybones' with their children, summarizing a narrative and its structure through a series of images. They referred to this when articulating the close relationship between children listening to stories and improving their writing:

> Using the storybones idea within the written work we found brilliant. They have to plan their stories in the SATs and we said 'why don't you do storybones?' ... I really do think that the children who struggled before got levels that were brilliant for them because they were actually able to write a complete story, whereas before they would get so tangled up in the middle ... I found as well that my reluctant readers, which were boys in my class, sort of didn't like to pick up a book but they loved the storytelling ... 'If we read some, we can do them in storybones and then we can tell them'.
>
> (Jo)

For Shirley, persistent tellings and retellings of traditional stories, when allied with teaching about 'storybones', offered scaffolding and models from which Year 6 children could develop their own writing. Previously, many members of the two classes:

> Had no shape to the stories they wrote. They have been told continuously that stories have a beginning, a middle and an end but ... they actually read novels and a novel is enormous ... There is no shape which they can use for a model. But traditional stories have a very definite shape and they can take that shape and they can use it. I think they have begun to realise that you have a beginning, you have a problem and you have a resolution and then it has an ending. I think really that has been the most significant thing that we used story for ...

Kae explained how, following storytelling and listening, the process of restructuring and embellishment of children's own written stories 'took a lot of work especially with the children who were less able and less happy using language'. The achievements of one particular Year 4 boy stuck in her mind:

> Some of my children really worked hard on opening sentences. To move from, because for one of my boys it was his first sentence, 'I went out' – to – 'Crash, bang the lightning went and we started on our journey.' It was a tremendous leap, an enormous move forward for him. It took a lot of putting down our ideas, writing our sentences, rewriting, refining, adding adjectives, saying it to partners, starting again. It was a long slow process but there was a purpose to it for them and that was the important thing.

MAKING CONTENT MEANINGFUL: TEACHERS AND STORIES

The TASTE project has used and developed stories across the curriculum, but as this chapter concludes we shall refer back to Edith Nesbit and the use of stories in teaching history. Nesbit, it will be remembered, participated in a long and, to some modern eyes, not entirely honourable tradition of educational storytelling. A century later, TASTE teachers and storytellers have been aiming at similar goals albeit through different routes. Louise's Year 1 and Year 2 children drew on family, friends' and neighbours' stories from the past to learn about oral history:

> They have also learnt that there is a lot out there, a lot of resources … that it is worth talking to people because people have got something to tell. They are quite surprised to find that their mummies and their daddies and nannies and grandads and aunties, have all got stories about things that happened to them or that they have been told; and that is something that is worth actually tapping into.

Kae echoes the findings of a recent national research project (Bage, Grisdale and Lister, 1999) with the comment that for her Year 3 and Year 4 children 'One of the most successful things we have done in the last two years is the Greek Myths. We have had our children sitting on the edge of their seats: tell us another one, another Greek Myth please. And they remember them.'

Meanwhile Shirley describes how two different sorts of story developed by Fiona Collins had captured her Year 6 children's historical imaginations. Firstly, a local legend about how Roesia de Lucy's heart had been buried in the Abbey at Abbeywood, by the Thames in Greenwich:

> They got a real feel for the Abbey, they got quite obsessed with it. We had an outing there … Once they got to the Abbey because they knew the story I couldn't believe how much they took in. Normally when you go on a visit with children they want to run about but the first thing they wanted to know about was where was Roesia's heart buried? What's here? Was the Abbey here?

Secondly, a documented story at the heart of English history … or should that be 'the birth'?

> She actually told the story of the Venerable Bede in the Abbey. Of all the stories I would have told my children, I would never have told them about the Venerable Bede. There she was going on about these Anglo Saxons … the first sort of history being written down. And they just hung on every word. Now to do that dry in a classroom you would lose them after thirty seconds: but they really took it in. It was an eye-opener for me … I would like to do more of that.

Educational accountability should perhaps centre upon what we remember, as well as do differently, as a result of teaching. Maggi, a Year 3/4 teacher from King's Lynn, describes how working with a storyteller like Hugh Lupton helped her children to 'remember' in fresh ways:

> The story is always the hook that the fact is remembered by. One of the main reasons I use story so much is that children will remember the story when they don't remember a list of facts. If you can hook it to a story line they pick up all the incidental knowledge that you want them to have and they don't realise they are learning.

For others, 'doing differently' implies that educational stories should change perceptions and balances of power, as well as improve skills in literacy or elsewhere in the curriculum. Drawing often from English examples, this American writer argues for the creation of a politically challenging and values-led canon of children's stories:

> The need for radical children's literature has never been so great. School, TV and casual conversation at home and on the streets are all silent on decency. There has never been a

period in my lifetime when it has been so urgent for children to know that there is more than one way to organise society, and understand that caring and cooperation are not secondary values or signs of weakness so much as affirmations of hope and life.

(Kohl, 1995)

Edith Nesbit might agree and although this is far from being the only aim of the TASTE project, so would many teachers within it. So, please remember next time you plan a lesson, a term, a target or a curriculum: teaching-as-storytelling offers more than just literacy.

REFERENCES

Applebee, A. (1978) *The Child's Concept of Story*. London: Chicago University Press.

Bage, G. (1995) 'Chaining the Beast? An autobiographical examination by an advisory teacher of whether spoken story telling and prompting can make school history's analytic transmission more educationally principled and powerful'. Norwich: UEA: unpublished Ph.D thesis.

Bage, G. (1999) *Narrative Matters: the teaching and learning of history through story*. London: Falmer Press.

Bage, G., Grisdale, R. and Lister, R. (1999) *Classical History in Primary Schools: Teaching and Learning at KS2*. London: QCA.

Callcott (Lady) (1878) *Little Arthur's England*. London: John Murray.

Collins, F. (1999) 'Bringing History Alive', in *Language Matters*, Spring. Southwark: Centre for Language in Primary Education (CLPE).

Dadds, M. (1998) 'Politics of Pedagogy'; paper presented to the Standing Conference for the Education and Training of Teachers (SCETT). Rugby: November 1998.

DES (1989) *National Curriculum English*. London: DES/HMSO.

DfEE (1997) *The Implementation of the National Literacy Strategy*. London: DfEE.

DfEE (1998) *The National Literacy Strategy: Framework for Teaching*. London: DfEE.

Egan, K. (1989) *Teaching as Storytelling*. London: Routledge.

Hilton, M. (1996) *Potent Fictions: Children's Literacy and the Challenge of Popular Culture*. London: Routledge.

Kohl, H. (1995) 'Should We Burn Babar?' *Essays on Children's Literature and the Power of Stories*. New York: The New Press.

Meek M., Warlow A. and Barton, G., eds. (1977) *The Cool Web: The Pattern of Children's Reading*. London: The Bodley Head.

Nesbit, E. and Ashley, D. (n.d.) *Children's Stories from English History*. London: Raphael, Tuck and Sons Ltd.

Robinson, M. (1997) *Children Reading Print and Television*. London: Falmer Press.

Sinclair, T. trans. (1962) Aristotle: *Politics*. London: Penguin Classics.

Vredenburg, Captain E., ed. (n.d.) *Children's Stories from English History*. London: Raphael, Tuck and Sons Ltd.

Wells, G. (1986) *The Meaning Makers*. London: Hodder and Stoughton.

White, H. (1987) *The Content of the Form*. New York: Johns Hopkins University Press.

II

Historical Narratives

Chapter 4

Storyseeds: Creating Curriculum Stories

Fiona Collins

STORYSEEDS

What is a storyseed? It is the germ of a story from the past, present or future; a story which might end as fact, fantasy or fiction; a story about a place or a person you know, or do not know, or think you might know. In the teaching-as-storytelling project (TASTE) in Greenwich, storyseed is the term which we have used to describe the starting points for a group of local stories. These stories, about local people connected with Greenwich at some point during the second millennium, also have global significance. The project, under the direction of Grant Bage (see chapter 3), took place in nine schools (seven primary, two secondary) in the London Borough of Greenwich, over the academic years 1997 to 1999. Each school nominated a teaching-as-storytelling co-ordinator, and these teachers received in-service training in storytelling techniques and strategies, as well as the opportunity to undertake postgraduate study on an aspect of the project of their choice. In each school one or two classes, normally including the co-ordinator's, became the focus groups for the project, and I visited them regularly in my role as the project research associate. My brief was, first, to work as a Storyteller in Residence, encouraging and developing storytelling and listening skills across the curriculum in both pupils and teachers. The second aspect of my role was to research and shape a group of local stories which became known as 'the millennium dozen'. The rich and varied history of Greenwich, combined with its unique, though shortlived, status as 'the millennium borough', made the development of the stories an interesting and challenging task. A range of starting-points was considered: geographical, chronological and cultural structures were all possible, but we came to the unsurprising conclusion that people were the most accessible and interesting focus. Both children and adults in the project began to look for starting points for stories, 'storyseeds', from which full blown tales would grow.

Two of the schools in the project are named after historical figures with local connections, so the names of the schools, Alexander McLeod and St Alfege, became their storyseeds. Another class, undertaking a local study, became curious about the name of Phineas Pett Road, where one of the children lived, and chose the street name as their storyseed. In one of the secondary schools students knew a whole host of ghost stories, local legends and urban myths about the nearby ruins of Lesnes Abbey, and these were combined with historical evidence to create a storyseed about the de Luci family and their connections with the Abbey during the 12th-century.

Further storyseeds came from my research at the Greenwich local history library at Woodlands in Blackheath. There I found a photograph and some newspaper clippings concerning Eliza Adelaide Knight, a suffragette and Fabian Socialist who lived in Woolwich at the beginning of this century. This evidence about her life grew into a story. I also found another reference which intrigued me, and which was to become the storyseed which is the focus of this chapter. Peter Fryer's history of black people in Britain (1984), included a reference to a black trumpeter who was employed by both Henry VII and his successor, Henry VIII. Henry VIII was born at Greenwich Palace and based his court there. The information that a solitary black musician had been working in the borough at such an early date was exciting, and a storyseed was created from the two extant pieces of historical evidence about this man. This chapter describes how a class of Year 5 and Year 6 children at Alexander McLeod Junior School worked with that evidence, using skills they had developed through the TASTE project, to create their own story about John Blanke the trumpeter, and to form their own relationships with him.

THE EVIDENCE

The first piece of evidence comes from the accounts of John Heron, the Treasurer of the Chamber to both Henrys, who recorded several payments to 'John Blanke, the black trumpet', the first of which is dated 7th December 1507. The GLC Ethnic Minorities Unit publication *A History of the Black Presence in London* (1986) notes that 'he had to wait a week for the 20 shillings due to him for the month of November 1507'. The second piece of evidence is pictorial, and comes from the painted roll of the 1511 Westminster Tournament, which was staged to celebrate the birth of a son, sadly short-lived, to Henry VIII and Catherine of Aragon. The Great Tournament Roll is in the care of the Royal College of Arms, and although it is too fragile to be on public view, its contents are accessible as a half-size reproduction in book form with an historical introduction by Sidney Anglo, who annotates this 'record of a great ceremonial' (1968). On the third and fourth membranes of the roll six trumpeters are shown, riding in two rows of three. Among them, according to Anglo's annotation, rides 'a negro (in the centre of the second row) who wears a brown turban latticed with yellow'. Apart from his turban, this trumpeter is dressed in the same yellow and grey livery as his bare-headed companions, and all six hold double curved trumpets decorated with 'the royal quarterings' to their pursed lips. Anglo notes that 'the black trumpet' listed in the treasurer's accounts was 'almost certainly the [one] depicted here'. The name Blanke, according to Anglo, was intended as 'an ironic jest', for it is, of course, related to the French 'blanc', meaning white. The group of trumpeters is shown twice on the roll, which is designed as a kind of single-frame cartoon strip, showing the procession to the tournament, the jousting, and the procession away again as a continuous pictorial narrative. On his way home the black trumpeter wears a different turban, but otherwise the musicians, shown on membranes 27 and 28, are unchanged. In this picture the caption above the trumpeters reads 'Le son des Trompettes. A lhostel', and Anglo notes that 'the cry *A l'hostel* traditionally announced the end of a day in the lists'. Only a few of the membranes from the roll are reproduced in colour by Anglo, but this is one of them, and I used it as the starting-point for developing this storyseed with the children of Kate Knox's class at Alexander McLeod School.

THE PROCESS

We began that process on 22nd October 1998 by looking closely at the full colour reproduction in Anglo's book. I read the extract from the treasurer's accounts and explained that this was all we knew about John. The children were full of questions: Where had he come from? Who were his people? What was his real name? Why and how did he come to England? What drew him to music, and specifically to the trumpet, as a way of making a living? When they realized there was no way of answering these questions they were first frustrated, and then excited by the challenge of developing their own plausible answers through story. We worked with a clear understanding that such answers could only be hypotheses, and that there is no longer any way of establishing 'the true story of John Blanke'. The history topic for the term was the Tudors, and children were soon drawing on and applying their own knowledge, and turning to non-fiction sources for evidence, in their quest to create a context for John's appearances at the Tournament on 12th and 13th February 1511. Because we were working from a visual image, I made the first task a graphic one and asked the children to create their own portraits of John. The class teacher and I encouraged discussion about John and his life as the children worked. We began to weave stories about this man, using talk, that most powerful medium of communication, and drawing, that most reflective medium. Twice I stopped the work in progress, the first time to ask children to share some of the comments and ideas about John which they had voiced to me as they worked, or had expressed through their drawings. Many of the pictures were formal portraits, showing head and shoulders, with liberal use of a generously shared gold pen on John's exotic turban. Some children had copied the Tournament Roll and showed John on horseback playing his trumpet. We all agreed that this must be a hard combination to execute skilfully, and this preoccupation was reflected in several of the finished stories. One boy had spent time trawling through the illustrations of a non-fiction book about the Tudors and was drawing John at home in his kitchen, surrounded by a wealth of Tudor domestic detail.

After sharing some of the ideas which were beginning to emerge, in order to enable more articulate children to model for others, I asked the children to continue with their individual or shared drawings, and to decide where their picture would fit in a storyboard of three frames. Storyboard, a technique borrowed from media studies, is a useful way of recording a story in pictures, like a strip cartoon. This strategy for remembering a story is an excellent memory aid for oral storytelling, because it fixes the key points of the narrative without recording them in written words, allowing the storyteller to improvize around the core of the narrative rather than recite from memory, as an actor does from a script. I had never before used it as a technique for creating a story, but now I drew a three frame storyboard on the board, and labelled the frames 'Beginning', 'Middle' and 'End'. I asked the children to decide where their picture came in such a storyboard; whether they had drawn the beginning, the middle or the end of a story about John Blanke. I left them with the task of drawing the other two pictures to complete their storyboard, thus telling a complete narrative about John in pictorial form.

I returned to the class on 17th November to help with the further development of the stories. I found that the work had progressed a great deal through Kate's teaching. She asked me to work on storytelling skills with the class as most of them had constructed narrative skeletons for their stories, which now needed 'fleshing out'. I began the afternoon by asking the children to take four minutes in small groups to remind themselves of the story so far: there were pairs, threes and fours working together. Some groups had completed their narrative and were able to summarize the whole story between them in this introductory activity. Others had developed only the beginning, so I asked them to tell up to the point they had reached. Then I asked them to work with mental images: each person in the group was to choose a location in their story, to picture it in as much detail as possible in their mind's eye, as if they were camera people, and then to describe it to their partner or small group. In this way, I aimed to build on and extend the graphic skills the children had used as a starting-point, by asking them to work imaginatively in a way which I knew from my own experience would feed into and enrich the oral language of their storytelling. We also worked on alliterative pairings of nouns and adjectives for the developing stories, in order to practise some oral traditions of language patterning. After this I asked the groups to polish their storytelling or complete their narrative, as appropriate. We ended the session by hearing the stories of three groups who volunteered to tell, and then receive feedback, in the form of positive praise on the content and delivery of their stories. This session consolidated and developed the work which had begun three weeks earlier, and left Kate with the achievable task of enabling the children to polish, present and record their narratives.

In mid-January Kate collected together the children's work on John Blanke's story and sent it to me. The bundle included drawings, 'passports' for John giving details about his life, notes for stories, written accounts, and taped storytellings made by the pairs and small groups who had devised the stories. A rich collection of stories had been spun around the two scraps of evidence which had constituted the storyseed. Drawing on the children's ideas, my own research, and traditional storytelling devices, I developed the story 'The king's trumpeter' to add to the 'Millennium dozen'.

THE PRODUCT: THE KING'S TRUMPETER

This is not a 'Once upon a time' story, because it is about real people, who really lived and died, but is not a history story either, full of dates and facts, because lots of the dates and many of the facts have been forgotten or lost. You'll have to decide for yourself how much of it is true, and how much has been made up, because even though I'm the storyteller, I don't know the whole story. Here's what I do know: the story of King Henry's trumpeter.

> Long, long, long ago, there was once a boy called John. He lived with his parents in a fine house in a small town somewhere on the golden coast of West Africa. He was apprenticed to his father as a carpenter. But in his heart he was a musician, always singing as he sawed

or smoothed or shaved. He played the drums, whistles – anything he could get hold of, teaching himself to play and picking out tunes by ear. His family loved his music, and they enjoyed many evenings of music, song and stories together.

In 1509 John's peaceful world suddenly came to an end. Perhaps it was fighting and war, or plague and famine, or the curse of slavery. We can never know why John left his home. They say he was 29 when he left. All he took with him into a different world was one bag of precious belongings, and his stories and music, which he carried in his mind.

He had enough money to pay for a sea crossing, but the ship that he took was old and rickety. It was a long and tiresome voyage, from harbour to harbour around the north-west coast of Africa, and then along the coast of Spain. He wasn't sure where he was going, and he wasn't sure if he was going to get there. He felt in his bones that something was going to happen to the boat. It did. The ship capsized and was lost off the coast of Land's End, Cornwall. John was a very strong swimmer and managed to swim to the shore, with his precious bag tied tightly across his shoulders.

The locals weren't too friendly at first. They knew nothing of black people, and made fun of him, calling him Mr Blanke (which means 'white' in the French which was spoken at the time). But John was gentle and ignored their taunts. He even began to call himself Mr Blanke, adopting the name they had given him in mockery and making it his own. And when he started to sing his old songs and tell his old stories, and especially when he taught himself to play the strange instruments of this new land, pretty soon they started to like him.

So time passed, as time does, and John became an expert at the new music he was learning. He especially liked the trumpet and often played it loud and long. Then news began to arrive that there was to be a Tournament in London, to celebrate the birth of the king's son, Prince Arthur. Musicians and other entertainers would be needed to make the day go well. John wanted to go there and play the trumpet for the king, but he did not know how he could make that long hard journey to London. But the locals had grown to like and respect him, so they raised money between them to help him on his way. John made that long journey, lifting up one foot and putting it down again, lifting up the other foot and putting it down again, all the way to London. John was very tired when he got there.

When he reached London and found the king's palace in Greenwich, he was told that there was to be an audition. He said to the king, 'Master, I am John Blanke and I have come to play the trumpet for you today. If you like my music let me play in the procession. I should like nothing better than to wear your livery and to be one of your trumpeters.' Henry VIII liked him because he seemed so different from the other musicians who were there, so he was given the chance to try out for the king's trumpeters. The king said, 'Very well, you can play.' John played his best pieces and the king was impressed, and offered him the job. John asked the king, 'How much would you pay me?' and the king answered, 'Four shillings a week'. John accepted the post.

He didn't know how to ride a horse; it was something he had never tried, but Henry VIII employed someone to teach him, and soon he was a master at it. He had a fine black horse of a silky shiny colour. John had to learn to play the trumpet on horseback, so that he could play and ride in front of the king in the Tournament procession. It was not easy, but he soon taught himself to do it. After all, as he said, 'If I could play on the rough sea crossing from my home to this land when the ship was rolling like a bauble in the storm, surely I can play while riding a sweet-tempered horse like young Beauty here.'

Finally, it was the day of the Tournament. John was nervous but he managed to play really well, and was the star of the Tournament. He played his heart out. He played like the sound of the birds in the morning. It was the best day of his life. Everyone crowded around to congratulate him, and his heart was full of joy.

John became one of the king's most favoured musicians, and lived a long and happy life at the King's court until the end of his days.

If you believe, you believe, and if you don't, you don't.

REFLECTIONS ON THE PROCESS

As a storyteller with a repertoire of traditional tales from around the world, I had never before been asked to create new stories, and I found the process problematic until I devised a way of involving the children in the storymaking. I was particularly concerned about the implications of mixing true facts and historical evidence with fabricated details, such as John's birthplace and family details in the exemplar above. Whenever I tell stories to children, of whatever age, and regardless of the flights of fancy contained in the story, the first question I am most commonly asked is: 'Is that a true story?' I am constantly impressed by the tenacity with which even the youngest children seek out truth. Perhaps a commitment to understanding the world in which they live underlies this question? I would never seek to pass off falsehood, fantasy or exaggeration as truth to children, who rely on significant adults to help them understand the world. Yet, without detail, stories would not ring true: the bare bones of the historical facts about John needed fleshing out if this was to be a story rather than a footnote in a text book. For children, details are often of more interest than the 'big picture'.

This fascination with detail was especially clear in the drawings: for example, in Lee's picture of John in his kitchen, with the trumpet hanging in pride of place in the middle of the wall, candelabras burning merrily, a dog lying beside the blazing fire and a very authentic-looking high backed settle where John could sit near the fire to warm his toes. It was also demonstrated in the oral stories which the child storytellers recorded on audio tape. For example, Frankie's notes for his oral story explained John's interest in music by describing how 'John's dad died of cancer. His father was a trumpeter before he died. John Blank wanted to trade the tridishon on'. (sic) Lisa and Nadine, who understood the importance of regularly practising one's instrument, decided that John 'played (the trumpet) every morning when he woke up and when he went to bed'. They also worked out that 'John's journey to London (from Turkey) took him eight weeks. He left in February and arrived in April.'

In my version of John's story I combined details taken verbatim from the children's stories with the clear narrative structure of a journey or quest, a motif so common to oral traditions worldwide that the notion of 'the journey of the story' has come to be used as a metaphor for the narrative itself. An over-riding concern was for the 'tellability' of the tale, and careful consideration was put into selecting vocabulary and attending to the aural rhythm of the story when told aloud. However, we had also planned to publish the stories as a set of Greenwich 'big books', and so more familiar considerations of sentence structure, readability and complexity were also taken into account in producing a final draft of John's story. But 'final' is a relative concept with an oral story, for it will be as the story is told and retold in the project and more widely that it will really take shape. The real work, the 'shaping by tongues', is yet to be done.

IMPLICATIONS FOR TEACHERS AND STORYTELLERS

There can be pitfalls in this way of approaching history teaching: there are dangers for the history, which may be lost from sight in the creative act of developing the story. There are also dangers for the storytelling process, for stories created for instrumental ends may become dry and dull if the joys of telling stories and playing with spoken language are buried under a preoccupation with the transmission of factual information. I still have, too, some misgivings about reaching a satisfactory conclusion to the 'is it true?' debate. But how many benefits may accrue if the process of developing a local storyseed into a tellable, engaging story is one which includes and empowers children at every stage!

Children can make real connections with people from the past through this storied work: the fine-grained intellectual and emotional skill of developing empathy, 'standing in another person's shoes', seeing another person's point of view, can all arise from the process of using information and imagination in recreating someone's story (Bage, 1999). In a way, empathy is a prior quality to accuracy in this process. Mistaken facts can subsequently be corrected through research, reference to primary or secondary sources, or gentle intervention by a teacher. On the other hand, caring about people who lived long ago, and wondering about the forces which shaped their lives, is a sensitising and engaging activity, which can lead to both a stronger cognitive engagement with history and a lifelong passion for it.

Furthermore, children engaging in the process of nurturing a storyseed are experiencing at first hand the power of the oral tradition in action, and making their own contributions to it. No story is ever told in exactly the same way twice: all storytellers have a right, which is also a duty, to tell the story in their own way. In the oral tradition, no one can tell you, 'You're telling it wrong', because of the importance of the performance aspect of storytelling: the creation of the story in the moment of telling, in the space between the teller and the listeners. In this ephemeral art form, a real equality of opportunity exists in which a child's contribution may be as valued and valuable as that of the most experienced storyteller. For those children who see themselves at the very bottom of the pecking order of achievement, the experience of contributing to the oral tradition on equal terms with adults, as happened in our work on John Blanke's story, is one which can powerfully boost their self-esteem, a quality which is eminently transferable to all other spheres of learning.

And the realization that aspects of their own storytelling, whether language patterns, characterization or events, can be incorporated into the stories of others is a powerful and direct experience of the oral tradition in action: the development of that nameless (at least in English) equivalent of the world's written literature; the corpus of oral storytelling to which every storyteller, of whatever age or ability, has the capacity to make a real contribution.

REFERENCES

Anglo, S. (1968) *The Great Tournament Roll of Westminster*. Oxford: Clarendon Press.

Bage, G. (1999) *Narrative Matters: the teaching and learning of history through story*. London: Falmer Press.

Ethnic Minorities Unit of the GLC (1986) *A History of the Black Presence in London*. London: Greater London Council.

Fryer, P. (1984) *Staying Power: the History of Black People in Britain*. London: Pluto Press.

Chapter 5

Venturesome Ways: Historical Fiction and the Novels of Henrietta Branford

Judith Graham

Children's historical fiction as a genre is slippery to define. Does it include period fiction such as the novels of Frances Hodgson Burnett and E. Nesbit which, for current readers, certainly create historical situations? Does it include biographies such as lives of Florence Nightingale or Christopher Columbus? Perhaps it should be confined to those books which are clearly based on available evidence? Many of Theresa Tomlinson's books start from accounts of the working lives of flither-pickers (1992) in Whitby, or of rope carriers in Derbyshire (1991), and she complements her stories with Frank Sutcliffe's contemporary photographs and relevant early 19th-century engravings. For some there is insufficient drama in these novels to qualify as fiction, so should we allow the opposite extreme and call Philip Pullman's *Ruby in the Smoke* historical fiction? It is set in Victorian times, he has certainly done his research into such areas as the opium trade and the early development of photography, but in the end do we read this as a romantic and thrilling page-turner and not as a seriously recreated historical situation? If we take so severe a view, we will have problems with time-slip fantasies which start in the present day and shift back to the past, though some of the most eminent children's writers have created much-loved books in this format, from Alison Uttley's *A Traveller in Time*, through Lucy Boston's *Green Knowe* books to Phillipa Pearce's *Tom's Midnight Garden* and Jill Paton Walsh's *A Chance Child*. Perhaps we think of historical fiction as that which creates for us a period for which few records exist and for which imaginative reconstruction is necessary? Much of Rosemary Sutcliffe's output and, more recently, Julian Atterton's work, fits this category. For many, the purest form would be the placing of a fictional hero or heroine (often a child) into an authenticated historical scene. Cynthia Harnett's *A Load of Unicorn*, set in Caxton's time, or *The Wool Pack*, set in 15th-century England with the wool trade in decline, or Geoffrey Trease's *Cue for Treason*, set in Shakespeare's time, would all come into this category. There have also been, recently, many examples of picture books which succeed in the creation of a story set in a convincing past. Can these be allowed as historical fiction? One thinks particularly of the work of Catherine Brighton, whose reputation rests on her recreation in words and pictures of the childhoods of Nijinsky, Mozart and the Brontes, and of the lives of children living through famous times such as the Great Fire of London or at the time of the disappearance of the Marie Celeste. And if these pass muster, then what about the Asterix books which supply a sense of the past for more than a few of us?

We are also troubled by trying to answer the question of where historical fiction starts and ends. The strictest ruling is that fiction becomes historical when it is about a time that no-one living can remember at first hand. At the end of 1999, this would exclude writing on almost every occurrence in the 20th-century. Others argue that yesterday is history and that indeed children's sense of history can best develop by moving into the very recent past and going back from there. Elizabeth Laird's *Kiss the Dust* covers eighteen months from 1985 to 1986 in Kurdish history but, with television and air-conditioning in the book, it does not feel like historical fiction. Robert Westall's *Gulf* similarly tells of a significant historical period but, with television images of the war and screen briefings, not to mention the presence of Saddam Hussein, it is not comfortably categorized with classic historical fiction such as Rosemary Sutcliffe's *Eagle of the Ninth*, set during the Roman occupation of Britain, or Henry Treece's early 13th-century novel, *The Children's Crusade*.

Historical fiction is not only difficult to define; it is difficult to discover its readership. All children's books need to be promoted and teachers are in the strongest position to influence. For historical fiction, this is a problem because it has to please two large and strong-minded groups of teachers. English teachers will not promote it enthusiastically unless they feel it reaches a narrative standard and a relevance that is achieved by contemporary or established 'classic' fiction. They know that their pupils want to read about characters more obviously like themselves, in terms of lives, clothes, customs. History teachers in their turn worry about accuracy and will not promote historical fiction unless the pay-off for the time spent is noticeably better informed pupils. In any case, they are faced with a curriculum in the 1990s that tends to undervalue 'empathy' and that asserts the importance of primary sources and direct evidence, rather than a talented author's manipulation and interpretation of that evidence. Both of these opposing views are encapsulated in these remarks of the historical novelist, Hester Burton: 'Historical novels ... are frowned upon by the Establishment. Historians look upon them with contempt, feeling sure that their authors must have tampered with ... historical fact. The straight novelist regards them as ... a misuse of their writer's talents. A novelist's duty is to portray life as he knows it – namely, in the contemporary scene' (Meek *et al.*, 1977).

Teachers are, in their turn, influenced by reviewers. Maria Cachia's review (1998) of Henrietta Branford's novel is typical, at least in its opening statement: 'An initial glance at the blurb of *Fire, Bed and Bone* filled me with dread. It was set in 1381 and centred on the Peasants' Revolt. Not being a fan of historical novels ... I approached with caution.' (The reviewers' prejudices were completely dispelled by the end of chapter one.) Many current reviews begin, 'Historical fiction may not be fashionable but ... ' or 'This fine young writer is committed to an unfashionable genre ... ' or 'Historical novels seem for some reason to be the poor relation in the field of children's fiction' and often include such phrases as, 'heavy-handed historical signposting' or 'slightly old-fashioned feel ' or 'the historical novel does not have the prestige it used to have'. Why should this be so?

Undoubtedly, there is prejudice. Many turn against what they view as a hybrid form. Many have memories of pre-war jingoistic novels which were full of swashbuckling and archaic language and resist the genre on principle. Geoffrey Trease claims that, when he started writing, 'there was a prejudice against historical fiction, which was associated with compulsory holiday reading' (Meek *et al.*, 1977). John Rowe Townsend writes (1990), 'the phrase 'historical fiction' may not ring excitingly in children's ears'. This statement suggests a resistance to the genre but he then adds, 'I do not believe that individual books, *if otherwise appealing*, will be resisted on the ground of being set in the past.' (my italics) In the work of Henrietta Branford and of certain other recent historical writers there is ample evidence of extra appeal. I shall try to examine wherein it lies.

In *The Fated Sky* (1996), Henrietta Branford treads bravely in Viking country where Rosemary Sutcliffe, Henry Treece and, more recently, Julian Atterton have notably been before. *The Shield Ring* (Sutcliffe, 1956), *Blood Feud* (Sutcliffe, 1976), *Horned Helmet* (Treece, 1963), *The Last of the Vikings* (Treece, 1964), *The Shape-Changer* (Atterton, 1985) have given this era good coverage. What is it that Henrietta Branford can add? Why is she 'otherwise appealing'?

The Fated Sky begins with a striking visual image of a dragon in the sky, flaming red with its jaws open. Ran, the sixteen-year-old narrator of the story, feels the eye of the dragon is watching her. 'I feared it,' she says. (The book also closes with this image but by then Ran is grown and she is not afraid.) All fiction needs to arrest its reader at the start. Branford not only gives us this symbolic image but her opening sentence, 'There was a dragon in the sky', concludes with 'the night before the stranger came'. We cannot miss the ominous connecting of these ideas. We are made to wait a page or two but then we see the stranger and, as this is a first-person narrative, we see him utterly through Ran's eyes.

> When I turned to run up the little slope to our house, there was a stranger there. He had jumped down from his horse and was standing with his back to the dawn and his face to our door. My mother stood in the doorway with the early morning light shining on her face, and he was staring at her. He put out a hand to touch her, then drew it back. She leaned forward a little, kissed him, and leaned back, as if to study what effect this might have on him. Because of the way he stood and looked at her, not moving, not speaking, full of longing, I saw her for the first time as a stranger might.
>
> (1996)

The dragon image, the sense of foreboding, the startling impact of seeing a parent objectively and, what is more, seeing her transfixed by a stranger who is surely bad news, combine to arrest the reader, but we may need still more than this. We must be willing to follow the protagonist. We must care about Ran. We must believe that Ran is cut from the same cloth as ourselves. Our sympathy is caught when Ran, in a desperate effort to deny the news of her father's and brothers' deaths that the stranger has brought, calls him a liar. For this, her mother beats her with a stick pulled from the pile of firewood and bans her from the house.

> 'Get out,' she hisses. 'If I'm to have no sons, I'll have no daughter either. Give your company to the beasts tonight. They will enjoy it more than I do.'

Our shocked sympathy is not quite enough however; we then listen to Ran's thoughts:

> I felt ashamed, ashamed of having been so rude. And stupid, too. If I had longed, secretly, for my father to return, how much more must my mother have longed to see her sons sail home again?

A child who has so much more understanding than that shown by her mother commands our respect and our interest. Undoubtedly, in addition, some readers will be anticipating the mother's downfall; they will not have long to wait. Now that readers will willingly travel with this character, the circumstantial detail which sets the historical period can be slipped in with freedom. Branford is still careful not to overload. Choosing to write in the first person is one way of keeping things light.

The Fated Sky is told in the first person, as are many historical novels, including several of the titles from which I quote below. First person narratives tend to restrict the volume of information and only display what is visible to and understood by the protagonist. The character's ignorance is thus the reader's, and the dawning implications can be revealed and parcelled out in a way which adds to dramatic tension. Hestor Burton, author of *Castors Away!*, writes, 'When I come to describe the historical situation I have chosen, I try to view it through the limited vision of a single character'. In *Castors Away!* she describes the Battle of Trafalgar through the eyes of the boy who has to run backwards and forwards bringing gunpowder to the ship's gunners. 'He has no more idea of the battle's significance or outcome than those actually present at the time.' (Meek *et al.*, 1977). Similarly, Ran in *The Fated Sky* has no overall perspective on the events unfolding but she gives us, her readers, information that we piece together into a coherent whole just as Ran does (or does not). On the other hand, the first-person narrator moves in many ways unseeingly through her world, taking many things for granted. The author cannot afford to allow Ran to describe too much of her ordinary life for fear of clogging the story with a mini-history lesson. Alun Hicks and Dave Martin amusingly show that the modern equivalent of 'Joanne . . . ran a wooden comb through her hair and cleaned her teeth with a hazel twig' would be along the lines of 'Joanne ran a plastic comb through her hair and picked up a toothbrush to clean her teeth'. (1997). If detail is determined by the genre rather than the needs of character and plot, the reader will tire and abandon the book. The two facets – of first-person ignorance and first-person immersion in a taken-for-granted world – are seen at work in these three short passages from *The Fated Sky*. After the death of her father, Ran, her mother and Vigut, the stranger, make a journey by sledge across Norway's snow-covered wastes between their home and Sessing, a neighbouring farmstead.

> Mother sat in front, under the great fur rug, with Vigut. They leaned in close to one another and talked; I could not hear what they were saying. My mother laughed a lot and so did Vigut. When his long hair blew across her cheek, she did not brush it away.

On this journey, Ran's mother is fatally wounded by a wolf. On arrival at Sessing, her mother is taken away to be tended.

> Vigut was standing by the table, drinking from a horn of mead. I saw his eyes over the rim of it, following the best-looking of the servant women. I went and stood beside him, waiting to ask him where my mother was. When he had finished drinking, he called the servant over and told her to refill the horn. Then he looked down at me. The mead was working fast on him; he did not try to hide his dislike of me.

'She's in the women's room,' he said eventually.

I didn't understand. At home we have one room, and it belongs to everyone.

Ran's mother dies and her funeral takes place.

The slaves picked up the bench, one to each corner, and carried it outside into the yard. They waited while another slave led Bor [their horse] out of the barn, Finulf following with a sharp knife in his hand. I had not known Bor was to be my mother's sacrifice.

In these three extracts, we can see how the perspective of the sixteen-year-old allows us as readers to continue with her unspoken lines of thought about Vigut and draw conclusions of our own. We know that Vigut is seducing Ran's mother and that he is a womanizer even though Ran does not directly tell us and may not know herself, though she can report external behaviour. Indeed, some readers may not draw these conclusions if they are reading this novel before they are ready for it. We are also able to appreciate that customs – such as grander farms having a room for women, waiting one's turn to speak, drinking from horns, sacrificing an animal at a death and burial without coffin – were commonplace to these people, as were fur rugs, travel by sledge, men's long hair, wolves and mead. We are not treated to an elaborate explanation of these details and rituals – we observe as Ran does, draw our conclusions and build up our secondary world. We may have to work quite hard but in the process we gain a clearer and clearer image of the times.

Henrietta Branford has another device to draw on later in the book when she creates the blind singer Toki for Ran to fall in love with. In the process of Ran's relaying of visual data to Toki and of Toki's explanations to Ran of how he manages without the power of sight, much information can be naturally introduced into the narrative. Thus, when Toki plans to take Ran to Vegasund, he shows her and her anxious Grandmother how he will find his way.

He took from the bottom of his sack many small parcels of cloth and hide. Each had a chip of wood sewn to it, and each chip was cut with runes. Toki read each one with his fingertips until he found the one he wanted. He opened the parcel and unwrapped the layers of cloth until what looked like a piece of chewed boot appeared. He held it out to Kon [his dog], who sniffed it thoughtfully, licked it, nosed it again, and barked. . . . 'I find something for him to smell in each new place I want him to remember. He'll always lead me back'.

The combination of the most basic animal instincts with the sophistication of a symbolic system (runes) lends authenticity here and strengthens the narrative at the same time. The runes mentioned have already been partially taught to Ran by Toki and will go on to play a vital part in the poignant denouement of the story. Toki's blindness also enables the author to have Toki taught to weave (women's work) and, when the two set up home together, Ran carries out traditionally male tasks, if they are tasks which require sight. Whilst such an arrangement may not have been typical, it is believably portrayed and will be readily accepted by 20th-century readers.

The choice of a girl as main character gives the book a special quality seldom found in books about this period. Throughout the book, the flow of Ran's experience – her grief that her mother did not love her, her parting from her grandmother, her sensuous falling in love with the blind harper Toki, the scenes of childbirth and miscarriage, her sympathy with the childless, her concern for the children trapped in the grain store – feels of its time and yet is of universal relevance, and an education in human sympathies for the modern reader. The battle scenes – compulsory in any Viking saga – are reported from Ran's viewpoint and focus on the fortunes of characters already known to us as she watches them meet their fate. Because we know that Vigut is leading the marauding forces, the tension is considerable, becoming almost unbearable when Ran has to watch Vigut approaching the unseeing Toki who is playing his harp and singing on a hill above the battle scene. The breaking away from the 'heroic tradition' with its inevitable male narrative viewpoint is undoubtedly one of the reasons why this novel is so refreshing and appealing. The decades of feminism since Rosemary Sutcliffe's first books have made an impact on the Viking novel.

The creation of tension has been touched on more than once in the analysis of *The Fated Sky*. It is here that the historical novel, in less expert hands, often fails. In Vigut, Branford has created a villain whose presence is asserted from the beginning. He and the cunning Brokk comprise a terrifying threat to Ran and Toki, especially after they have thwarted Brokk's attempt to poison and sacrifice Ran. After their journey from Norway to Iceland, Ran and Toki are allowed three chapters of fulfilment and happiness, before Ran finds evidence in a belt with a wolf's head clasp that Vigut is also in Iceland. Toki's reassurances give her, and us as readers, little comfort. Then clues are dropped into the weft of the story – talk is passed on to them of fighting in the North by men, hungry for land. Then we hear that their leader has a wolf's head on his shield. And so the tension mounts. Few historical novels control development and denouement as finely as Branford does here. Even the battle being suddenly ended by a volcanic eruption – possibly stretching credibility – is acceptable, because the narrative seeds of this have been sown earlier in the book. One is inclined to say that the more gripping the adventure, the more history is absorbed.

There is one more aspect of historical fiction we must consider, that of language. In the years since Geoffrey Trease wrote, 'Ye olde jargon must go', thinking as he was of such 'pishtushery' as 'I joy me', 'Wot you what?' and 'Thou shalt taste the sting of the lash, young varlet' (Meek *et al.*, 1977), the writers of historical novels have mostly avoided doomed attempts to try to capture or convey in any accurate way the English spoken in the period they are covering. Few writers can equal the achievement of Rosemary Sutcliffe or of Jill Paton Walsh who, through an immersion in the contemporary written language, whether it be sagas, chronicles, letters, records or literature, manage to make us believe that they have heard the authentic language rhythms of the period. Peter Hollindale speaks of the 'close verbal echoes' of surviving Eyam documents that Paton Walsh incorporates into the 'gravely beautiful language' of *A Parcel of Patterns* set in the plague year of 1665. Here is Mall at the end of the story:

> I walked down Eyam street like a stranger, as though I looked upon it as I had seen it never before, and came to Sydalls' house, of which the door stood wide, with coltsfoot growing free upon the threshold. I stepped within, staring all around. Grass grew up through each chink between the floor-flags; the pewter plates and pans were tarnished

dark, the kettle flecked with rust, and in the garden windows spiders spun screens of web all thick with dust.

(1983)

Here is Paton Walsh again in *Grace*, the story of Grace Darling:

Mother . . . climbed up, and she could not see us. She saw the great ocean running in waves half as high as the tower, and not a sight of the coble. All round her the massy glasses and reflectors of the lantern glowered in the black storm-light like quenched coals and below she saw the heaving water buck and sink, so that her eye could find no level and it seemed the tower itself was keeling over and still no sight of the boat.

(1991)

And here is Rosemary Sutcliffe in *The Shield Ring*:

The wind rose and wuthered against the deep thatch, making the flames of the torches jump so that one moment the hall would be plunged in shadow, and the next the light would leap upward, playing on the smoke-dimmed shields that hung from the house-beam and bringing the snarling mask of the ancient figurehead leaping forward out of obscurity; then sinking so that all the hall was lost again save for the flame-lit ring of warriors about their leader's body.

(1956)

No-one does it better than these two, yet Branford's prose seems right for her Viking story; it comes magnificently into its own as she tries to convey the delirious state into which Ran is thrown by the poison administered to her by the evil Brokk, before the sacrificial murder he is planning.

Brokk pushed the neck of the flask between my teeth and tipped it up, filling my mouth and throat with scalding, burning fire. I choked and spat and swallowed until the flask dangled empty in Brokk's white hand, and sight and sound and smell spun me off my feet and up high somewhere above the roof beams, from where I would look down and watch my going. Brokk began to twist his snakeskin rattle and my mind spun and my heart jumped with its patter. Toki struck a chord on his harp, and the sweet sound of it billowed out across the smoky hall, driving Brokk's darkness out, sending it racing through the door and out into the night. I saw Brokk running with it like a spider, out into the snow, and still he stood over me, the empty flask dangling from one hand. Shape-shifter, I thought. Magician. I saw the torchlight burnishing his spear, and the shadow of the rope writhing like a serpent into the great tree outside in the yard. I saw it raise its head and twist its tail into a noose, while Toki's chord beat like the wings of a swan, and his voice leaped like a silver fish mounting the bright steps of a waterfall to spawn, singing to me of light and life and freedom.

(1996)

The passage itself seems to twist between life and death, good and evil, with Brokk and Toki each fighting to claim Ran for themselves. As always, it is not only the language itself that is capable of conveying psychological truth so appropriately, but also the placing of such passages at key moments in the book. Another moment is the heartbreaking leave-taking of Ran and her grandmother Amma, encapsulated in these words at the end of a chapter:

> We ate and drank and pretended to be safe, which no one is, of course. We let the warmth of the fire and the shelter of the old house and the love of Amma draw the long aching of the road out of our bones.

Whilst there is nothing here about the language that is particular to the Viking era and the Viking era alone (and how do we know how they really spoke? and in any case, if we did, we would have to translate their language), there is nothing so strained and self-consciously archaic that the reader is alienated. The subtle echoing of slightly different rhythms, the use of vocabulary more Anglo-Saxon than Norman, and the judicious use of images tied to the life and landscape of the era under question all play a part in the creation of a convincing secondary world without losing readers along the way.

If Henrietta Branford has been adventurous in her first-person female narrator in her Viking novel, she has been doubly bold to take a female dog as her narrator in the second novel I shall consider, *Fire, Bed and Bone*. Henrietta Branford is not the only historical novelist to have seen advantages in taking an animal as narrator. *The Journal of Watkin Stench* (Meredith Hooper) has the rat Watkin as narrator and through him we appreciate the horrors and hardships of the early settlers in Australia. In situations where the lives of animals and humans are interwoven, and where animals have in many ways more mobility and freedom, to select an articulate animal as narrator is a shrewd decision.

Fire, Bed and Bone is set in 1381 at the time of the Peasants' Revolt. One quickly adjusts to the choice of a domesticated hunting dog as narrator, and the advantages of selecting so unconventional a narrator emerge once one has accepted the conceit. Just like a child narrator, the dog can puzzle, question and only slowly reveal her understanding of the tricky historical and political situation, gradually phasing in details. Other aspects – the presence of wolves, wild boar, the straw bedding, the children sleeping with their parents, the horse living inside, the earth floor – affect the dog as much as the humans around. As these everyday conditions are included and revisited, so a picture of the times is built up. In addition, the dog (who is never named) has one great advantage as narrator, in that she has the freedom to roam and can report on the state of the outside world and move deftly between locations and people. As she claims, 'I am a creature of several worlds'. Indeed, she approaches the omniscient narrator role at times but without the detachment that that suggests. We never forget her dogginess – or her sense of humour – as is evident in this extract, which is centrally important for the reader's appreciation of the role of the preacher (who could be John Ball) in inspiring the peasants.

> The younger people would rather have been dancing, but they listened. Out on the fringes of the groups, we dogs drowsed, and scratched for fleas.
>
> 'Do you believe', the preacher asked, 'that God made the poor to be the servants of the rich?'
>
> Nobody answered. The preacher's dog caught a flea, cracked it between his teeth, and glanced up at his master.
>
> 'What did he make Adam? Rich man? Poor man?'
>
> Still nobody answered.
>
> 'I will tell you', the preacher said. 'I will tell you what the Bible says about it.'
>
> The preacher's dog shut his eyes. He'd heard it all before.

A second device used by Branford is to have the dog's master, Rufus, married to a woman, Comfort, who is very much younger than he. His first family has died in one of the first plague years. Comfort is cast as ignorant of the root causes of the peasants' unrest. Through the long cold winter and spring whilst the dog is perforce housebound, nursing her puppies, the dog listens to and reports on Rufus's explanations to his inquiring wife, which, in the process, gives Branford's readers the essential background to the era's harsh economic conditions and resentments.

> 'There is trouble coming. It comes from the great plague, Comfort, as flies follow rubbish to the midden. The plague killed so many, labour was scarce, good fields were left untilled. Poor folk like us began to know our worth and ask for better wages.'

The age difference between husband and wife eventually, I think, makes it easier for readers to accept Rufus's death when it comes. In the extract that follows, which tells of Rufus's hanging, the dual focus – the event and the dog's involvement – also helps to soften the sorrow the reader feels.

> The scaffold was already set up in the square, the crowd gathered below. The midwife fought her way through the people and took the children from Comfort, so that they should not see their father die. She tried to take Comfort away too but Comfort would not go. She stood still in the crowd until it was over. I held close to Comfort, pushing my nose into her hand, pressing my warmth against her legs, telling her I was there.

The Fated Sky broke new ground by giving a picture of the lived experience of a young girl in Viking times. *Fire, Bed and Bone* also has an utterly different feel from many historical novels in that the dog's experience of finding food, mating, giving birth, coping with the separation from her puppies and their deaths, the knowledge of the hardships that befall her son, all shape and permeate the other story of the peasants Rufus and Comfort, their family, their enemies and their fates. The dog's awareness of the unsafe world they all share is properly channelled through its nose for much of the book; astonishingly, this seems to have relevance to the human lives in the story. (And I have to add that for some time after I had finished this book, I felt my own olfactory processes heightened.) The lives of dogs and humans are so closely paralleled that the book constantly and convincingly reminds us how close to the land, to the seasons, to danger and misfortune we all used to live. It is a measure of the book's power that this atmosphere is absorbed without apparent imaginative effort. It is also a measure of the book's impact that it left me feeling better informed of the historical situation. Indeed the couplet,

> When Adam delved and Eve span
> Who was then the gentleman?

seemed more elucidated by this novel than by anything else I have ever read. What is more, it sent me off to read more about the Peasants' Revolt and though I acquired much information and many names and dates in other places, I have Henrietta Branford to thank for creating a memorable picture of the past, and one that remains as a mental icon to be contemplated again and again, as is the way of stories.

It also sent me off to find her latest book, *White Wolf*, which I had seen reviewed. The review ended with the words, 'One sore point though. This book is an illustrator's dream. So why aren't there any illustrations?' (Gardiner, J. *Times Education Supplement*, 20 November 1998). There is obviously a role for illustration in historical fiction. Cynthia Harnett illustrated her, still wonderfully readable, historical novels with her own line drawings and C. Walter Hodges was his own illustrator for his stories of Columbus, King Alfred and Elizabethan theatre. Their work adds greatly to the store of our historical images. Many of the 'golden age' historical novels (I am thinking of the period from about 1954 to 1969) by such writers as Ronald Welch, Frederick Grice, Rosemary Sutcliffe, Hester Burton, K. M. Peyton, Barbara Picard, Geoffrey Trease and Henry Treece were illustrated by leading artists. It is impossible not to recall Brian Wildsmith's pit-head scenes in Frederick Grice's *The Bonnie Pit Laddie* or Charles Keeping's powerful work for Rosemary Sutcliffe's and Henry Treece's Roman Britain novels or Anthony Maitland's atmospheric drawings for Leon Garfield's novels. Victor Ambrus is the superb illustrator for a score of writers and Garth Williams's work for Laura Ingalls Wilder's *Little House on the Prairie* books is also invaluable in its contribution to our understanding of those times. Regrettably, illustrating historical fiction is no longer common; it is expensive for publishers and yet not particularly lucrative for the illustrator.

Picture books have to some extent absorbed the talents of today's top illustrators, and picture books set in the past are as finely researched by their illustrators as they are by their authors. P. J. Lynch's illustrations for the 19th-century *The Christmas Miracle of Jonathan Toomey* (Susan Wojcieska) or for Amy Hest's *When Jessie Went Across the Sea* most certainly help children to imagine buildings, interiors, clothing, transport and occupations. I have also touched on Catherine Brighton's fine period evocation, and Michael Foreman, Roy Gerrard and many others make historical picture books hugely informative and alluring. A sense of period is aided by illustrations; of that there is no doubt. But there are dangers; Kath Cox and Pat Hughes tell of a child who decided that the Napoleonic story *Seeing Red* (Sarah Garland and Tony Ross) 'could not be true' because Tony Ross's quickly sketched people 'don't look real' (1998).

In the end, the novelist can actually go beyond specificity and give us an education in human understanding; for that, pictures are not compulsory. I am an ardent fan of illustrated books but spending time with the unillustrated fiction of Henrietta Branford has been an adventure that has required only her great competence to jump-start my imagination. I cannot believe that it could be otherwise for young readers, as long as the books reach them. Fortunately, *Fire, Bed and Bone* has been awarded prizes that have brought it to a wider audience than usual. It may well herald the start of a new life for the historical novel where story, with all that that means in terms of creating characters whose lives are caught up in exciting plots, and respect for the spirit of known historical evidence are imaginatively combined. Such novels should find favour with children, teachers, historians and literary folk alike.

BIBLIOGRAPHY

Children's Books
Atterton, Julian (1985) *The Shape-Changer*. London: Julia MacRae.
Branford, Henrietta (1996) *The Fated Sky*. London: Hodder.
Branford, Henrietta (1997) *Fire, Bed and Bone*. London: Walker Books.

Branford, Henrietta (1998) *White Wolf*. London: Walker Books.

Boston, Lucy (1954) *The Children of Green Knowe*. London: Faber.

Garland, Sarah and Ross, Tony (1996) *Seeing Red*. London: Andersen Press.

Grice, Frederick (1960) *The Bonnie Pit Laddie*. Oxford: Oxford University Press.

Harnett, Cynthia (1951) *The Wool Pack*. London: Methuen.

Harnett, Cynthia (1959) *A Load of Unicorn*. London: Methuen.

Hest, Amy and P.J. Lynch (1997) *When Jessie Went Across the Sea*. London: Walker Books.

Hooper, Meredith (1992) *The Journal of Watkin Stench*. London: Piper.

Laird, Elizabeth (1991) *Kiss the Dust*. London: Heinemann.

Pearce, Phillipa (1958) *Tom's Midnight Garden*. Oxford: Oxford University Press.

Pullman, Philip (1985) *The Ruby in the Smoke*. Oxford: Oxford University Press.

Sutcliffe, Rosemary (1954) *Eagle of the Ninth*. Oxford: Oxford University Press.

Sutcliffe, Rosemary (1956) *The Shield Ring*. Oxford: Oxford University Press.

Sutcliffe, Rosemary (1976) *Blood Feud*. Oxford: Oxford University Press.

Tomlinson, Theresa (1992) *The Flither Pickers*. (second edition) London: Walker Books.

Tomlinson, Theresa (1991) *The Rope Carrier*. London: Julia MacRae.

Trease, Geoffrey (1940) *Cue for Treason*. London: Blackwell.

Treece, Henry (1958) *The Children's Crusade*. London: The Bodley Head.

Treece, Henry (1963) *Horned Helmet,*. London: Brockhampton.

Treece, Henry (1964) *The Last of the Vikings*. London: Brockhampton.

Uttley, Alison (1939) *A Traveller in Time*. London: Faber.

Walsh, Jill Paton (1978) *A Chance Child*. London: Macmillan.

Walsh, Jill Paton (1983) *A Parcel of Patterns*. London: Viking Kestrel.

Walsh, Jill Paton (1991) *Grace*. London: Viking.

Westall, Robert (1992) *Gulf*. London: Methuen.

Wilder, Laura Ingalls (1937) *Little House on the Prairie*. London: Methuen.

Wojcieska, Susan and Lynch, P.J. (1995) *The Christmas Miracle of Jonathan Toomey*. London: Walker Books.

REFERENCES

Burton, Hester (1977) *The Writing of Historical Novels*, in Meek *et al.*

Cachia, Maria (1998) Fiction Reviews, in *The English and Media Magazine*, no. 38, Summer 1998.

Cox, Kath and Hughes, Pat (1998) *History and Children's Fiction*, in Hoodless.

Gardiner, Josephine (1998) From Predator to Free Spirit, *Times Educational Supplement*, 20 November 1998.

Hicks, Alun and Martin, Dave (1997) Teaching English and History through Historical Fiction, in *Children's Literature in Education*, Vol. 28, no. 2, June 1997.

Hollindale, Peter (1997) 'Children of Eyam: the Dramatisation of History', in *Children's Literature in Education*, Vol. 28, no. 4, December 1997.

Hoodless, Pat (ed.) (1998) *History and English in the Primary School*. London: Routledge.

Meek, Margaret, Warlow, Aidan and Barton, Griselda (1977) *The Cool Web: The Pattern of Children's Reading*. London: The Bodley Head.

Townsend, John Rowe (1990) *Written for Children* (fifth edition). London: The Bodley Head.

Trease, Geoffrey (1977) *A Lifetime of Storytelling*, in Meek *et al.*

Chapter 6

The Long Road to Canterbury: Children's Chaucer

David Whitley

The BBC's broadcast of a new, animated production of six stories from Chaucer's *Canterbury Tales* shortly before Christmas in 1998 makes this a timely point to review what Chaucer may mean for children at the end of the 20th-century. What value do the *Canterbury Tales* have six hundred years after their composition? In what forms have they been made available to contemporary children? And to what extent are the issues which have exercised academic debate as to how Chaucer should be understood reflected in the versions which children can read and view today?

The issues raised in trying to answer these questions may seem specific to a single writer, but their implications are actually of central importance to debates currently raging over children's literature. The tag which often accompanies Chaucer as the 'father of English poetry' gives his writing unique status within the canon of English literature as the origin, or source, of the creative streams which followed. Chaucer's stories therefore have a particular significance and position within debates about the value of a literary canon and the contexts within which children may (or may not) be introduced to canonical writing. Moreover, the language in which the *Canterbury Tales* were written, which looks so different from modern English and requires effort to understand, intensifies the terms of this debate, since there has been an implicit assumption that the 'authentic' Chaucer is only accessible in texts with the original Middle English language and spelling conventions. Hence, in terms of literature encountered in schools, Chaucer has been given central status as an obligatory text on most 'A' level courses, yet has not, in the main, been considered suitable for younger children.

Recently, however, there have been great interest and heated discussion amongst English teachers at all levels of the education system, about the ways in which texts change in the process of transmission between different cultural contexts and historical periods. Chaucer's writing is a particularly rich site for such interest since so many of his stories were already 'rewrites' of pre-existing narratives. Indeed the image of what Chaucer was about has changed quite radically over the centuries. In all kinds of ways then, 'versions of Chaucer' are currently ripe for investigation, and the kind of Chaucer which is available to children is of particular importance.

The perceived need to maximize 'authenticity' in readers' encounters with texts of the *Canterbury Tales* has undoubtedly exerted more pressure on the way versions of Chaucer have been produced than has been the case with many other canonical writers whose work has found its way into children's literature. Swift's *Gulliver's Travels*, for instance, and Defoe's *Robinson Crusoe* (to cite just two examples from many possible) have proliferated in various versions – bowdlerized, abridged, rewritten, illustrated, repackaged in chapbooks and eventually 'Disneyfied' – from relatively early dates in their histories. Even Shakespeare, whose cultural status has stimulated a more than usually intense demand for fidelity to the 'original' text, has endured fewer restrictions than Chaucer in this respect.

A quite different set of priorities has driven successive productions of Chaucer's best known masterpiece. It was one of the first books to be printed in England, which widened its cultural dissemination, but the rapid rate of change in the English language, particularly during the 16th-century, meant that its linguistic forms were already archaic by the time Spenser was writing in the Elizabethan period. By the end of the 17th-century the *Canterbury Tales* was sufficiently inaccessible to the non-specialist reader for John Dryden to produce the most famous of the early modernizations. Dryden reproduced only three of the tales and saw it as a virtue that he had refashioned the stories to suit the tastes of his own age. 'I have not tied myself to a literal translation'; he wrote in his Preface, 'but have omitted what I judged unnecessary, or not of dignity enough to appear in the company of better thoughts'. From the late 19th-century onwards, however, the prestige associated with the scholarly text of Chaucer has ensured that the vast majority of new translations have aimed to stay as close as possible to the perceived original. Although there have been attempts, particularly in the 20th-century, to perform, dramatize and even produce musical adaptations of a selection of the tales, these have been largely against the grain of dominant practice in schools and colleges, where the study of scholarly editions in Middle English has predominated, often rather reluctantly supplemented with the easier reading of 'faithful' translations into modern English.

The effect of this tradition of textual transmission and reading practice can be seen even in 20th-century versions designed explicitly for child readers. Eleanor Farjeon's popular mid-century rendering, for instance, first printed in 1930 and reissued in a new edition by Oxford University Press in 1959, was specifically aimed at developing, as she put it, 'a taste for Chaucer in young people'. Yet such was the drive towards preserving a sense of integrity in relation to Chaucer's intentions that, even though the volume was entitled *Tales from Chaucer*, Farjeon decided to reproduce *all* the *Canterbury Tales* in the precise order prescribed by the most authoritative editorial opinion known to her. In her preface of 1930 she justifies this decision on the grounds that 'to keep the Pilgrimage intact, every tale told by Chaucer must have its place; the interludes and personalities would become far less rich and amusing if any man in the fellowship had not his say'. The view of the *Canterbury Tales* which emerges here is of an organic whole which must be kept intact and which is held together by the dramatic interactions and psychological traits of characters ('interludes and personalities'). This view is very much in line with the theories advocated most influentially by Professor George Kittredge in the early years of the century, which came to dominate much academic criticism of the *Tales* up until the 1960s. Kittredge believed that the tales were essentially performances which revealed much about the characters who told them and that the sequence as a whole was held together by the drama of the pilgrims' interactions with each other. Yet, though it is in tune with mainstream academic criticism of her day, Farjeon's version of the *Canterbury Tales* presents real difficulties as an attempt to capture the imagination of young readers and inculcate a taste for Chaucer.

Many of these difficulties arise from the decision to include all the tales in the sequence. The problem which confronts many writers of children's versions of the *Canterbury Tales* – what to do with gross or bawdy elements derived from the medieval genre of fabliau – is here writ large. Whereas other writers can at least choose which of the fabliaux they think are amenable to reworking in a form suitable for children, Farjeon has to take the full weight of Chaucer's prolific creative interest in rude stories. Thus the tales attributed to the Miller, Reeve, Merchant, Shipman and Summoner all have to be reproduced in forms which 'handle with care' (or frankly omit) elements to do with sex or bodily functions that children are not supposed to talk about: the result is a parade of curiously bowdlerized and seemly stories. Only the Cook is spared this treatment, since Farjeon takes advantage of the tradition established in some early manuscripts where the Cook tells the 'Tale of Gamelyn' (the story which was to serve as the basis for Shakespeare's *As You Like It*). Modern editors have unanimously rejected the view that 'Gamelyn' could have been written by Chaucer but at least this tradition gets Farjeon out of one of her difficulties. She can include a whole, and thoroughly proper, story from the Cook and also omit the more authentic fragment Chaucer was developing for this character, which ends famously and abruptly with the cameo portrait of a wife who (literally translated) 'fucked for her living'.

I will return later to the issue of how writers handle the coarser elements of Chaucer's comic vision. But it is worth noting, before moving on from Farjeon's version, that the decision to include all the tales leads to an even greater problem in sustaining the enthusiasm of a child readership. The volume must take on board Chaucer's (albeit, for his time, restrained) commitment to medieval sermonizing. In particular, the long moralizing allegory which constitutes the 'Tale of Melibeus', and the fully fledged sermon contained in the 'Parson's Tale', are both included. While it is true that readers can always elect to skip anything they find uncongenial (even if they are advised that the effect of the whole is much diminished if 'any man has not his say') it is nevertheless a strong testimony to the power of prevailing theories of authenticity in determining how literature *should* be read, that such unpromising material, from a modern child reader's perspective, should have been included.

In addition to making choices as to what to include from the whole corpus of the *Canterbury Tales*, any new version of the tales is likely to reconfigure the qualities of the implied author who has conceived and orchestrated the stories. This is especially the case with the *Canterbury Tales*, of course, because Chaucer included images of himself both as writer of the tales and as one of the participants in the pilgrimage. In the General Prologue he promises to provide a description of each of his fellow travellers 'so as it semed me', sounding, characteristically, a keynote of subjective judgement in all that follows.

The differences between the kinds of author who emerge from different versions of the *Canterbury Tales* are closely tied up with the way Chaucer's work as a whole has been valued and the reasons which have been offered for why he should continue to be read. In the century or so after his death, Chaucer was valued primarily as a master of rhetoric, a man who showed an exemplary skill in handling language in its most formal, figurative and persuasive registers. After the Renaissance and the Reformation there began to be a stronger appreciation of the critical but understanding eye Chaucer cast on his fellow men and women and on society as a whole. This tendency reached its apotheosis in the image of Chaucer consolidated towards the end of the 19th-century. In this view, Chaucer was represented as a wry commentator on the human comedy and condition. His wisdom was associated with an acceptance of a variety of perspectives on human experience, a liberal tolerance sharpened with a keen, but ultimately benign, sense of irony. More recently, as the liberal consensus within humanities has been extensively challenged and the 'wisdom' of revered texts has come to be seen as a focus for deconstruction rather than celebration, Chaucer's irony has come to seem less stable and more pervasive than appeared before. Irony in this most recent view, rather than being seen as a key term in the expression of Chaucer's humanity, is seen as the form in which he allows for the interplay of competing discourses.

I am aware that this broad sweep has involved some vast, and rather incautious, generalizations, and apparently moved us some distance from any recognizably 'children's Chaucer'. But what I intend is to bring into focus a tension that has underlain much of the academic writing on Chaucer in the latter half of this century. The tension is between the image of an author committed to realizing a particular kind of humane balance and wisdom through the art of storytelling, and the contrasting image of a writer whose value lies in his questioning of all forms of received authority, the wielder of an ultimately unresolved scepticism. Some of the best recent criticism has contained elements of both these positions, however, and I am arguing here that the ensuing debates are more relevant to children's versions than might at first appear.

Consider, for instance, the 'Knight's Tale' which all the modern children's versions I will consider here retain as their opening narrative, despite very considerable variation in other respects. The way the image of Chaucer's Knight has been perceived illustrates in itself how readers have increasingly subjected all forms of authority in the *Canterbury Tales* to a pervasive, destabilizing irony. The consensus which previously operated in relation to the tone of the Knight's portrait in the General Prologue (even so vehement and sharp-eyed a critic of imperialism in all its guises as William Blake took Chaucer's Knight to be the universal 'guardian of man against the oppressor') has come under pressure since 1960, as some critics have begun to see in it varying degrees of ambiguity (Mitchell, 1964), anachronism (Howard, 1976), and even outright criticism (Jones, 1980). The 'Knight's Tale' itself is perhaps more problematic even though it is regarded by most critics as one of the finest of the tales. The problem, as so often with Chaucer, lies in interpreting and responding to its tone. The outline of the plot is conventional enough and the characterization is (unusually for Chaucer and presumably deliberately) remarkably thin. Two young knights and cousins, Palamon and Arcite, who are imprisoned, both fall in love with a beautiful girl called Emily whom they see in a garden through the bars of their prison. When, after much suffering, they are freed to pursue the object of their adoration, they fight over her and are recaptured by Duke Theseus, who had first imprisoned them. Theseus allows them to settle their rival claims on Emily by formalizing their conflict in a grand tournament. Arcite wins the day at the tournament but, in a cruel stroke of fate, is thrown from his horse during his victory parade and dies. Palamon eventually marries Emily and they live happily.

The main line of the plot is straightforward enough and the characters are so little developed that many readers find it impossible to distinguish between Palamon and

Arcite, the competing young knights. The real interest and depth in the story comes from Chaucer using the plot to express a philosophical attitude towards suffering and the apparent arbitrariness of fate. It is the working out of the terms of this philosophy within the storyline which constitutes the austere but deeply felt power of the tale for adult readers. Yet herein lies a problem for writers who wish to reproduce the tale for younger readers. The philosophical standpoint needs a slow-moving, ample narrative structure to unfold its resonances fully (Chaucer's tale is over 3000 lines long). Stripped of this amplitude, the philosophy collapses into a rather superficial stoicism mixed with conventional romance. The austere, grave undertones of the fuller version are not generally attractive to young readers whose experience of the world has not yet normally encompassed the hardest aspects of fate. Hence most writers reduce the length of the tale and soften the edge of its uncompromising philosophy. The risk is that the characters will then be exposed in their thinness, and that for grave philosophy will be substituted slight charm.

Geraldine McCaughrean's version (1986) tries to solve this problem by extending the range of opportunities for ironic readings of the plot and characters. The thinness of the characterization and the conventionality of the romance plot thus become a pretext for a version which borders on burlesque. The following excerpt will give something of the flavour:

> Down in the garden, Duke Theseus' young sister-in-law, Emily, had come to gather flowers in a wicker basket. She sang as she picked them – and the flowers seemed to turn up their faces towards her, and to faint at the touch of her hand.
>
> 'Oh lady! I'll wear your favour until the day I die!' said Arcite breathlessly to himself.
>
> Palamon pulled the stool away, and they both fell in a heap on the floor. 'What? Are you making fun of me, Arcite? It's serious! I'm in love with her!'
>
> 'You? You didn't even think she was human! It's I who love her.'
>
> 'You Judas! You cuckoo! Where are your vows of lifelong friendship now? The first chance you get you stab me in the back. You ... you ... '
>
> 'Viper! You thieving magpie!'
>
> This undignified scene was interrupted by the gaoler bringing in their one frugal meal of the day. 'What's this, puppies?' he said setting down the tray.

This, it must be said, is pretty lame stuff. The attempt to find a modern idiom for Chaucer's courtly love scenes to which children can relate results in a burlesque bordering on pantomime. While it is true that Chaucer's original provides hints of absurdity in its handling of the lovers' conflict, to push the absurdity this far is to lose contact with any serious undertones, to dumb down the plot for the sake of some rather limp comedy. It is possible that the decision to adapt the story in this way owes something to the attitudes I identified earlier as characterizing late-20th-century Chaucerian criticism. This tale could be taken as an extreme form of Chaucerian irony played out against convention and authority – in this instance the authority of idealized conventions of love. Although the adaptation is unsuccessful here, there is some support for this view in another of McCaughrean's innovations, the decision to break up the storyline (and challenge the authority of the imagined storyteller) with a pause offering an opening for commentary from the audience of pilgrims:

'Which do you think was better off?' mused the Knight, thoughtlessly interrupting his own story. 'Was it the man in prison or the man in exile?'

'Lord love you, have you no spark of wit?' demanded the lady I recognized from the night before by the enormous size of her hat. 'If the boy in exile had one half a brain, he'd disguise himself and go back to Athens. If all he can do is sit around and mope, he doesn't deserve the woman!'

'Well, well,' said the Knight, rather taken aback by the strength of her feelings. 'That's just what happened.'

Undercutting the authority of the single storyteller and foregrounding the interplay of different voices and perspectives (a strategy creating effects that literary theorists have called 'polyphonic') are qualities which have been praised in Chaucer recently, particularly by critics interested in applying Bakhtin's ideas (for example, David, 1976; Knapp, 1990). McCaughrean tries to recover a more serious tone in later parts of the tale, where the tragedy of Palamon's death is given some emotional power, reinforced by the swirling violence of Victor Ambrus' illustrations. But the return to burlesque at the end (Emily's reluctance to marry being registered through her graphic distaste for Arcite's physical appearance in the manner of recent feminist parodies of fairy tales) seems to me misjudged. One of the least successful of McCaughrean's tales, this version is more interesting for the ideas which influence its innovations than for the actual result.

Other recent redactors of the tales for children have generally opted for a more restrained approach to the 'Knight's Tale', abridging fairly drastically, but trying to keep some of its tonal balance. Selina Hastings' (1988) version handles the love scenes particularly well, her relaxed prose style nicely counterpointed by the formality of design in Reg Cartwright's illustrations. Ian Serraillier (1979) is very effective in the compelling gravitas which he manages to draw into the battle and death scenes. However, perhaps the most successful of recent versions in managing the tale's difficulties is the 1998 BBC animation. The principle here was to construct as much as possible of the dialogue and narration from lines taken directly from Chaucer. New lines linking or introducing scenes were used only sparingly, though the translations into modern English were free enough to allow colloquial ease and vividness in dramatic characterization. Each episode was screened twice, once in Middle English and once in modern, an interesting approach to the issue of authenticity. In the performance of the Middle English version, the visual text, of course, was able to provide massive support for viewers in quickly picking up the tone and meaning of the unfamiliar language.

Although in the BBC version the 'Knight's Tale' is reduced in scale to the common format of 8 to 10 minutes' viewing time, the larger context and resonances of the story are given dramatic force by amplifying the role played by the gods. The tale opens with an image of the gods' massive, half-human forms framing a globe, itself spinning within a cage of encircling bars. The theme of fate comes across with almost tangible force in this version as the supplication of each of the principal characters to particular gods is retained as a ritual re-enactment of the drama at the centre of the narrative, while in the climactic episodes the gods are *seen* continually intervening in human affairs. Another gain which the animated medium makes available is in the representation of the human characters. In the hands of first-class animators these characters can be rendered individually expressive but also distanced as symbolic 'types': the medium of animation is indeed particularly effective in creating an appropriate mixture of artifice and realism.

Many of Chaucer's stories centre on different forms of battle or contest between the sexes (he was described by one of his early admirers, Gavin Douglas, as 'women's friend'), so it is perhaps not surprising that gender issues should have featured particularly prominently in recent Chaucer criticism. Late 20th-century versions of the *Canterbury Tales* for children have, however, shown considerable variation both in the degree and the form in which they have taken such issues on board. Ian Serraillier's 1979 version, for instance, appears (for its time rather anachronistically) almost wholly impervious to any new thinking about gender. Serraillier embellishes his text of the 'Franklin's Tale' with such old-world wisdom as this, appended to the description of Dorigen's distress while Arveragus is away: 'She wept, she pined for him, as good wives always do when their husbands are away'. (Chaucer's line more interestingly attributes the propensity to pine for one's absent partner to the *will* of the noble woman concerned: 'As doon thise noble wives *whan hem liketh*'.) Serraillier again plays fast and loose with Chaucer's ascription of will in that *locus classicus* for gendered approaches to Chaucer, the 'Wife of Bath's Tale'. He opens the story with the knight seducing rather than, as in Chaucer, raping the young lady. In this he offers stronger meat than Geraldine McCaughrean's version however. She seems strangely ill at ease in the romance form and once again uses burlesque to smooth over the more uncomfortable issues in the narrative:

> The lady blushed. 'How prettily the water glistens in the brook.'
> 'Almost as sweet to taste as a kiss of your lips', said the knight, and he helped himself to a kiss. The lady picked up her green skirts and swooped like a parrot in and out of the trees, all the way back to the Court.
> So the over-romantic knight was summoned before the assembly of the Round Table.

It is hard to see how this 'over-romantic' knight could have earned the judgement of his peers at court that he should be put to death after this little episode. Fantasy seems to have given way to hysteria. Writing four years after McCaughrean, Selina Hastings is characteristically more straightforward and frank:

> Long ago, back in King Arthur's time, there lived a Knight known for his love of pleasure. Riding by the river one day, he met a pretty girl walking by herself and, ignoring all her pleas, he threw her to the ground and raped her.

McCaughrean was heir to a bowdlerizing tradition in relation to Chaucer texts for children which even Serraillier, in 1979, had done little to resist. Serraillier in fact had largely ducked the issue by including none of the fabliaux in his collection of tales, apart from the rather low key 'Shipman's Tale' from which the sexual elements could be pruned with relatively little loss to the sense of the story. By the 1980s, in a climate of much more open dialogue between children and adults over sex and bodily issues generally, this tradition was well overdue for radical overhaul. Although earlier texts had undoubted strengths in many areas, the bowdlerizing tradition placed severe limitations on what could be done with many of Chaucer's most acclaimed and fascinating stories.

In terms of handling Chaucer's more licentious stories with both tact and vigour, the audio-visual medium has advantages. Contrary to expectation, a visual text can sometimes be allusive, without avoiding an issue, where the verbal medium must either become explicit or coy. The recent BBC production of the 'Merchant's Tale' illustrates this point particularly well. The visual medium enhances the graphic undercutting of the would-be adulterous couple's romantic intentions when we literally see May tear up her *billet doux* from Damian and throw it down the opening of a primitive privy. Likewise, when the old merchant January becomes blind and, driven by obsessive jealousy, insists on his young wife accompanying him everywhere, May's sense of humiliating entrappedness is made palpable when we see her forced even to go to the toilet with her husband. Yet in the famous scene in the pear tree (in which Chaucer's most explicit verbal rendition of sexual coupling – 'this Damyan/Gan pullen up the smok and in he throng' – is a *tour de force* in terms of comic realism and timing), the visual text can be curiously discreet without losing vividness or impact. Here the actual coupling takes place off camera, the focus remaining resolutely on January at the bottom of the pear tree, while the cascade of golden pears which drop down the screen after May has made her ascent are quite enough of a semiotic for the adult viewer to imagine the frantic movement and spasms of sexual pleasure above. Indeed January's blind unawareness both of the shower of pears and of the coupling provides an additional, subtle piquancy to the hilarity of the scene. This is a particularly effective deployment of the visual text, allowing children and adult viewers to respond to the scene fully from perspectives appropriate to their age and understanding. It is a text which, rather than shielding children, allows them to understand more, on their own terms, when they are ready.

I began by suggesting that this was a timely moment to review versions of Chaucer and what they may offer children. It is also, I think, a fine period for versions of the *Canterbury Tales* of real quality and vitality to be produced. The relative openness and more extensive knowledge of young children today, in terms of sexual and bodily awareness, mean that writers have more freedom in handling the range of Chaucer's stories. In addition, artistic as well as technological developments in animation and audio-visual media generally have opened up exciting new ways of handling some of the difficulties, as well as the potential interest, of the tales. I have tried to establish some of the ways in which children's versions of Chaucer are informed by aspects of contemporary academic criticism. In some ways this is not surprising, since many writers who take up Chaucer have themselves studied English literature at university or have knowledge of at least some contemporary scholarship. The recent BBC production also drew on the very considerable knowledge of scholarly debates about Chaucer of Professors Jill Mann (1991) and Derek Brewer (1973). The real test of academic knowledge and debate is the extent to which it feeds into a living culture as well as drawing on a dead one. The creative energy and imagination which have gone into recent versions of Chaucer for children deserve a serious and informed response – one that recognizes the nature of the challenge which Chaucer's writing possesses, but also the pleasures and new understandings that may result from creative re-engagement with these old stories.

PRIMARY SOURCES

Dryden, J. (1700) Preface to *Fables Ancient and Modern* from *The Poems and Fables of John Dryden* (ed. by J. Kinsley, 1970). Oxford: Oxford University Press.

Farjeon, E. (1963) *Tales From Chaucer*. Oxford: Oxford University Press (illustrated by Marjorie Walters).

Hastings, S. (1988) *A Selection from the Canterbury Tales*. London: Walker Books (illustrated by Reg Carter).

McCaughrean, G. (1986) *The Canterbury Tales*. Oxford: Oxford University Press (illustrated by Victor Ambrus).

Serraillier, I. (1979) *The Road to Canterbury*. Harmondsworth: Penguin.

Myerson, J. (screenplay) (1998) *Geoffrey Chaucer's The Canterbury Tales*. London, Cardiff, Moscow: BBC.

Middle English quotations from Larry D. Benson (General Editor, 1988) *The Riverside Chaucer*. Oxford: Oxford University Press.

REFERENCES

Brewer, D. (1973) *Chaucer in his Time*. London: Longman.

David, A. (1976) *The Strumpet Muse: Art and Morals in Chaucer's Poetry*. Bloomington and London: University of Indiana Press.

Howard, D. (1976) *The Idea of The Canterbury Tales*. Berkeley, Los Angeles and London: University of California Press.

Jones, T. (1980) *Chaucer's Knight: the Portrait of a Medieval Mercenary*. London: Weidenfeld and Nicholson.

Kittredge, G. L. (1951) *Chaucer and his Poetry*. Cambridge, MA: Harvard University Press.

Knapp, P. (1990) *Chaucer and the Social Contest*. New York and London: Routledge.

Mann, J. (1991) *Geoffrey Chaucer*. Hemel Hempstead: Harvester.

Mitchell, C. (1964) 'The Worthiness of Chaucer's Knight', *Modern Language Quarterly*, 25, 66–75.

III

Visual Narratives

Chapter 7

The Art and the Dragon: Intertextuality in the Pictorial Narratives of *Dragon Feathers*

Tina L. Hanlon

Contemporary picture book artists weave stories and styles from past traditions of art history through the pages of their colourful books in many fascinating ways. There are non-fiction books that tell children the true stories of artists and their work, such as Diane Stanley's illustrated biography of Leonardo da Vinci (1996). Ruth Craft has built a verse narrative around details from Pieter Brueghel's painting *The Fair* (1975). Others, such as Nancy Willard's *A Visit to William Blake's Inn* (illustrated by Alice and Martin Provenson, 1981) and *Pish, Posh, Said Hieronymous Bosch* (illustrated by Leo, Diane and Lee Dillon, 1991), contain fanciful fictional tributes to artists of the past. Some intertextual links with the styles of past artists or trends in art history are purely visual. In *The Balloon Tree* by Phoebe Gilman (1984), the evil archduke and the princess's little dog look exactly like Giovanni Arnolfini and the dog in the well-known double portrait of Arnolfini and his bride by Jan Van Eyck (1434), while a painting on a palace wall appears to be a Madonna Enthroned in the style of Northern Renaissance painting. Paul O. Zelinsky's *Rapunzel* (1997), a recent winner of the Caldecott Medal, and *The Nativity* by Ruth Sanderson (1993), both feature lavish illustrations derived from Italian Renaissance paintings and architecture. Most of these artists maintain a consistent style throughout as they adapt older artistic patterns to the narrative designs of their contemporary picture books.

Other artists illustrate tales of fantasy and folklore by mixing styles within the same narrative, alluding directly and indirectly to artistic movements of the past, with strange and intriguing results. One such book is *Dragon Feathers* (Dugin and Dugina, 1993), an award-winning retelling of a European folk tale in which the quest of a poor wood-cutter's son involves acquiring advice and three feathers from a dragon. Eleven scenes on double-page spreads trace the hero's journey to the dragon's palace and back to his village to marry the bold and beautiful Lucy, daughter of the rich innkeeper who hoped in vain that the evil dragon would eat this unsuitable suitor. This is the second picture book by artists Andrej Dugin and Olga Dugina, a husband-and-wife team from Moscow. They adapted some of the same imagery and expanded the striking artistic techniques they had used in *The Fine Round Cake* (Esterl, 1991), a retelling of an English folk tale about a runaway Johnny-Cake. In the first book elegant borders and circular designs arranged in expansive white spaces add symbolic and dramatic dimensions to the narrative as the strangely anthropomorphic round cake flees across the pages from one scene to another. He is pursued by characters in Northern Renaissance dress, until the crafty aristocratic fox who devours him wanders smugly away, with her long gown trailing out of the final empty border. In *Dragon Feathers* the colourful illustrations on each double-page spread bleed to all four edges, giving the reader the impression of viewing magnificent paintings in a museum. Both books were published in Germany and then in English translations. The Dugins, like Gennady Spirin and a number of other Russian authors and artists who began their careers in the restricted cultural environment of the Soviet Union, turned to children's book illustration to acquire a livelihood and greater artistic freedom. Since the introduction of *glasnost* in the mid-1980s, they have been able to collaborate with international editors, bringing the tradition of lavish illustration in Russia to the attention of readers around the world (Mestrovic, 1991; Solomon, 1991).

In *The Best Children's Books in the World* (1996), a collection in which *Dragon Feathers* is reprinted, Jeffrey Garrett (1996) asserts, 'There is no such thing as an international children's book'. I agree with Garrett that many readers need to encounter more books from other countries, appreciate their origins in a unique time and place, and refrain from assuming that classic books in English reflect universal childhood tastes because they are translated and sell well in many other countries. From another perspective, however, I would argue that *Dragon Feathers* is an international picture book. It not only results from international collaboration among artists, translators, editors and publishers, but it also reflects international influences that have shaped European art and folklore for a thousand years. While the book jacket asserts that it is a folk tale from Austria's Ziller Valley, variants of the tale are familiar in many other regions. The Grimm Brothers' version called 'The Devil with the Three Golden Hairs' is reprinted in Jane Yolen's collection of world folk tales (1986), where she notes that this is 'one of the most studied tale types in the world.' Three hundred variants have been found all over Europe, and in diverse cultures in China, Africa, and North America. This story from a specific region in Austria, related to so many similar tales around the world, has been adapted by Russian artists in a book published in Germany and other countries. Its detailed oil paintings, like the texts of so many European and American folk tales, blend elements of ancient folklore and mythology with Christian symbols, scenes of ordinary domestic life and natural landscapes, adapting the iconography of previous storytellers and artists. The rich intertextuality in this combination of styles and images represents a contemporary awareness that, as folk tales are retold through history, their narratives often retain the surface illusion of simplicity, yet they reflect multiple dimensions of the various cultures in which they are retold.

The predominant style in the scenes depicting the village and the hero's quest is realistic, similar to Northern European art of the fifteenth and early sixteenth centuries. In particular, the Dugins' paintings pay homage to Pieter Brueghel the Elder and Albrecht Dürer. In the first scene, a face within the inn's doorway could be a portrait of Brueghel. Henry, the handsome hero, looks like a self-portrait of Dürer in 1493, at age 22. Dürer's initials, which happen to be the same as those of Andrej Dugin, are etched on a rock in the second scene in the same way that Dürer signed his paintings and drawings. Portions of the names of Dürer and his assistant, Baldung Grien, are written on a scroll and inside a wooden tub on later pages. The monograms of artists Lucas Cranach, Martin Schongauer, Matthias Grünewald, Lucan von Leydon and others also appear in the illustrations. Many details of landscape, costume and domestic life, down to floor tiles, folding wooden shutters, and basins within rooms, imitate realistic images in innumerable Northern Renaissance paintings (see Figure 7.1).

Perry Nodelman (1988) has noted the influence of Renaissance realism in the richly detailed fantasy settings created by many 20th-century fairy tale illustrators. Most extraordinary in *Dragon Feathers* is the combination of unrealistic details depicted in a realistic style. In both the scenes of rural life and the dragon's palace, there are bizarre images that call into question the relationships between the natural and supernatural, good and evil, human and animal life, animate and inanimate objects, verbal text and visual art. Some readers observe at once that the little fantasy creatures strewn throughout the book, beginning on the cover, endpapers and title-page, might have jumped off a canvas by Hieronymous Bosch. In Bosch's *The Temptation of St Anthony* (*c.* 1500), for example, there are fish bodies in strange positions, blended with other figures; eggs of different sizes; a creature with a musical horn for a nose; one with an owl on its head; and a little dog in a jester hat. These are similar to unrealistic images in *Dragon Feathers*, where animal, human, and angel bodies are merged with mechanical devices such as bagpipes, wheels and candlesticks.

Although Bosch is best known for using the most obscure and grotesque iconography in his 'puzzle paintings,' the landscapes and domestic scenes as well as the religious pictures of Brueghel, Dürer, Schongauer and other Renaissance artists are also full of narrative details and symbolism that the Dugins have borrowed. For example, Dürer's engraving of *The Prodigal Son* (*c.* 1496), like the village and farm scenes in *Dragon Feathers*, features lifelike images of pigs, roosters, weatherbeaten buildings, a protagonist who has been travelling with a walking stick, and a wagon wheel in the yard, a symbol of good luck in Northern Europe. Even the cow's rear end at the side of Dürer's picture is a realistic but odd detail, and *Dragon Feathers* contains some strange images of animal rear ends. In one of Dürer's most famous allegorical engravings – *Knight, Death and Devil* (1513) – the devil's swine head and horn, his cloven hoof, the hourglass and the knight on horseback are similar to details in *Dragon Feathers*. Brueghel's early painting *Netherlandish Proverbs* (1559) dramatizes dozens of proverbs in one crowded village scene. The inverted globes and prominent flag with a crescent symbol are some of the same ambiguous images associated with the sorcerer dragon in *Dragon Feathers*. Just as Erasmus collected proverbs in writing around 1500, Bosch and Brueghel recorded them visually to draw attention to human folly, and also used puns in their pictures. The Dugins may be playing with a popular saying by giving Henry such prominent, dangling bootstraps, while none of the other realistic figures wears such big boots. Perhaps they indicate that Henry is the self-reliant poor man who can pull himself up by his bootstraps. Or perhaps they hang so loosely because he does not have to struggle alone as he strides confidently through his quest and receives magical help.

'Reading' the art in this book is much like reading modernist poetry, or an allegorical Renaissance painting. The strange juxtapositions of unusual images seem illogical and confusing on the surface, but there are detectable layers of intertextuality and artistic patterns in the design of the pictorial narrative. There is symmetry in the arrangement of the plot and illustrated scenes. Before and after the central episode in the dragon's palace, complementary village scenes begin and end the narrative, while three pairs of parallel scenes depict Henry's journey out and return home with the three

Along the road Henry passed a cottage where a farmer sat crying and moaning, his head buried in his hands. "Why are you so sad?" Henry asked.

"My daughter has been ill for many years, and only one so wise as the dragon could help her, but—"

Henry interrupted, saying, "I'm on my way to the dragon's castle. Perhaps I can ask him what to do. I'll tell you what he says when I return."

feathers. The consistent figure of the attractive and valiant travelling hero unifies illustrations containing many mysterious images. For example, as Henry nears the dragon's palace, trees that become more strangely gnarled and twisted look nearly human at times, reminiscent of Arthur Rackham's early 20th-century illustrations of anthropomorphic fairy tale trees. As the introduction to *Dragon Feathers* in *The Best Children's Books in the World* states, 'These unusual features give the book an unsettling surrealism, recalling a more enchanting and fantastical time, when things did not necessarily occur with reason' (Garrett, 1996).

Rackham's and the Dugins' trees often contain birds depicted realistically or with some fantasy element like a little hat. The use of feathered things is a prominent example of the complex intertextual interplay of realistic and symbolic details which add layers of meaning to the narrative of *Dragon Feathers*. The spectrum of images associated with the aristocratic dragon displaying his magnificent multi-coloured wing feathers ranges from angels with brightly coloured wings as in medieval and Renaissance paintings, to the chickens that represent domestic life and prosperity. Both roosters and eggs, from the giant eggs in a nest near the farmer's house and at the wedding feast to smaller egg images in the dragon's palace, could symbolize Christian resurrection and creation, or lust and the pride of male heroes and alchemists. The rooster on top of the village gate as Henry leaves is there again, accompanied by a cherub, at the wedding. The village church spire is topped by a rooster instead of a cross. Mythological, sexual, domestic and Christian images are combined as they are in Bosch's and Brueghel's paintings.

The significance of the church spire is challenged further in the opening scene by the unicorn with an unusually tall horn positioned in front of it. Many other vertical images also have traditional associations with Christianity and/or earthly preoccupations such as sexual and economic power, from the tall dragon himself and the vertical architectural lines of his palace, to the tree branches, staffs, pikes, flagpoles and candlesticks associated with woodcutters, saints and warriors in Renaissance art. Henry the woodcutter's son carries a long, rough walking stick and he is surrounded throughout his quest by wooden images that link him with worldly heroes as well as saints, including St Joseph the carpenter and St Christopher with his tall walking stick.

All these symbols of male power and social hierarchies are rivalled by the dragon's wife with her impossibly tall pointed headdress and flowing veils. Ironically, these pointed hats or hennins that demonstrated the lady's indulgence in attention-seeking worldly adornments were sometimes called steeples; this extraordinarily high one contrasts with the church steeple and unicorn's horn, as well as making the lady into an imposing figure that rivals the tall dragon on the cover and within their palace. Her white skin and lack of hair around the face also give her an unearthly or eerie look, yet these were marks of beauty recorded in many Renaissance portraits and she is friendly, like her counterparts in other variants of this folk tale, as she tricks the dragon and helps the human hero. It is also ironic that the scene in which she greets Henry is reminiscent of many depictions of the Annunciation, in which Mary on the right under Gothic archways is approached by the angel on the left. In particular, the kettle and towel in the dragon's palace are very similar to details in Renaissance paintings of the Annunciation and the Nativity, where they are both realistic domestic images and symbols of purity. The hanging towel is identical to one in the Annunciation scene by the Master of Flémalle (*The Merode Altarpiece*, *c.* 1425–8), but in the dragon's magical house the kettle is hovering in mid-air in an open window, not hanging from a chain in an alcove. The encounter between the human and the supernatural has quite different implications in this tale of man versus dragon. The dragon's lady greets Henry with a rather provocative gesture and leads him immediately upstairs (see Figure 7.2).

Inside the dragon's palace, details reminiscent of Italian Renaissance style are blended with architectural patterns of columns, stairways, arches, and checked tiled floors that violate principles of realistic perspective, as in the popular modern artwork of M.C. Escher, who played with concepts of perspective and patterns of symbolism developed in the Renaissance. At one point Henry is hidden behind a window that is on the wrong side of the stairway; only his hand on the railing is visible as he follows the dragon's wife up the ornate staircase into a mysterious world where he hides under the bed. These sophisticated images of aristocratic life are juxtaposed with the rocky mountain cliffs outside the windows, in which the palace is almost embedded, and the huge gnarled trees and river that dominate the landscape as Henry approaches the dragon's domain.

In the midst of allusions to high art, esoteric mythological symbols and mysterious images of landscape are comic details such as the figure of the lustful dragon in his red nightcap in bed; he is separated by a page break from his wife on the other side of the bed, still adorned in her ridiculously tall steeple as she passes a dragon feather to the woodcutter hiding under the bed. The draperies of the dragon's bed resemble those in Van Eyck's *Arnolfini Double Portrait* (1434), a very famous 15th-century painting of newlyweds that combines domestic realism and a multitude of symbolic details. Similar bed hangings also appear in Renaissance scenes from the life of the Virgin Mary.

Although the spectacular dragon appears in only two poses in the centre of the book as well as on the cover, he is connected with smaller images of snakes, dragons and other creatures scattered throughout the narrative. Allusions to St George and the Dragon reinforce the theme of the Christian hero confronting the forces of evil. The dragon's one cloven hoof, green colouring and exceptionally long reptilian tail link him most explicitly with ancient images of the devil. His palace is full of allusions to ancient sorcery, or specifically to alchemy, such as eggs, crescent moons, funnels, bellows, flasks and open illuminated books. Renaissance artists exposed the depravity of alchemists who tried to tamper with nature, sexuality, creation, magical transformation and divine knowledge. Although the dragon's palace is not as disorderly or chaotic as the alchemists' studios depicted by earlier artists (such as Brueghel in *The Alchemist*, 1558, for example), many of the same implements are strewn around it. On the other hand, another popular Renaissance subject, St Jerome's study, contains many comparable features to depict a monk and scholar's life of devotion and study. In Antonella da Messina's *St Jerome in his Study* (1460), a row of arches in the background is identical to some arches in the dragon's palace. The architectural frame with symbolic birds and objects on the sill in the foreground is also similar to the Dugins' design of the scenes in the dragon's palace. These complex visual allusions to traditional stories of both sin and piety add depths to the hero's quest, building on the tale's intertextual links with other ancient narratives about human encounters with dragons and devils.

On the journey to the dragon's palace, a ferry ride across a river with a tormented fisherman, who is forced to serve endlessly as a ferryman while sacred figures kneel in prayer on the riverbank, confirms that this is a hero's epic journey to hell and back.

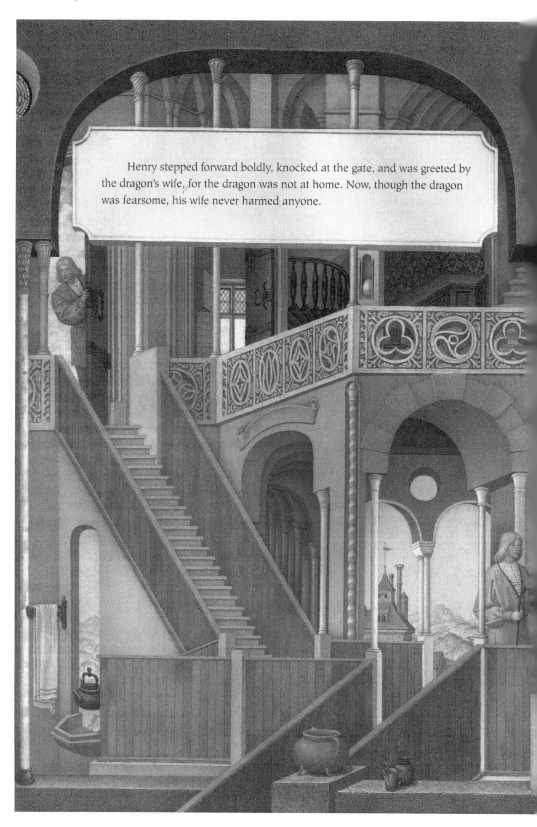

Henry stepped forward boldly, knocked at the gate, and was greeted by the dragon's wife, for the dragon was not at home. Now, though the dragon was fearsome, his wife never harmed anyone.

"How may I help you, kind sir?" she asked.

Henry explained his love for Lucy, the task set by her father, and the woes of the sick girl, the apple tree, and the fisherman.

"No human may speak with the dragon; he eats them all," replied the dragon's wife. "But come and hide under our bed, and keep your ears open. The things you wish to know, I will ask him," she said gently.

Wooden erections that could be signposts suggest crosses and gallows, while hooded figures on the edges of some scenes imply the presence of Father Time or Death. On the return journey the hero is able to rescue the fisherman, restore a barren apple tree to fruitfulness by killing a snake, and cure the farmer's sick daughter. These details allude to powerful biblical and mythological narratives of punishment for sin, death and rebirth, yet, as in many folk tales, the happy outcomes – the fulfilment of earthly human desires – are made possible by the hero's luck in encountering a magic helper, and the wife's ability to outwit the predatory dragon. Death is avoided while the present generation is empowered to enjoy life. In these scenes details such as kneeling figures of different sizes, knights and nuns, and elaborate coats of arms refer to the iconography of Renaissance art with its combination of secular and sacred symbols.

Even the gestures of pointing throughout *Dragon Feathers* link these illustrations to Renaissance paintings. In the return visit with the farmer, Henry points into a monochrome quatrefoil inset that reveals the poison stone under the sick daughter's bed. John the Baptist uses exactly the same gesture to point to Christ in Matthias Grünewald's haunting *Crucifixion* (*c.* 1510–15), while an angel points similarly to the Christ child in Leonardo da Vinci's well-known *Virgin of the Rocks* (*c.* 1485). In Lucas Cranach's *The Holy Kinship* (1510–12) a man points to a child's book in the same manner. These pointing gestures and images of keys scattered throughout the pictorial narrative draw us into the mysteries of intertextuality and interpretation that this book holds. A metafictional layer of symbolism also appears in the images of scrolls, with and without inscriptions, and of books found throughout the illustrations, sometimes in realistic contexts and sometimes in unlikely places. On the title page one dwarf writes in a book while another dwarf points as if to instruct him. As in avant-garde Russian artworks of the early 20th-century, mysterious numbers and floating alphabet letters on several pages suggest 'the visual expressiveness of letters, . . . a preoccupation with the dynamic possibilities of typographical form' (Paley, 1991). The other-worldliness of the dragon's palace is emphasized as the verbal text moves onto architectural structures on the walls; then in the dragon's bedroom, the text appears on shapes that look like scrolls of old parchment hanging like draperies. A baby dragon tail emerges from one end of a cradle, but there is a book where we would expect to see a baby head. The esoteric written and visual symbols throughout the illustrations, including the artists' monograms, are all visual clues drawing attention to the mythic and literary traditions that have produced this folk tale, and to the book as an artistic and literary artefact.

The crowded, rollicking wedding scene at the end occurs on the same spot where the narrative began, viewed from the opposite direction. The authoritarian father looming over the first scene has been eliminated; Henry tricked him into seeking the dragon to get more money for himself, while many symbolic details demonstrate that the couple who stand in his place are spending their wealth on a celebration of holy vows and physical enjoyment. The bulging purses and keys worn by humans and dwarfs in earlier scenes show the material success of the hero; as he acquires monetary rewards his purse becomes bigger and purse images start to appear on coats of arms, culminating in three purses on the new sign over the inn at the end. Bagpipes are found in realistic Flemish celebration scenes such as *The Peasants' Wedding* (1568) and *The Wedding Dance* (1566) by Brueghel, and they are associated with shepherds in Northern Renaissance Nativity paintings, yet by the 17th-century they also represent excessive revelry and phallic symbols in Northern European iconography. Brueghel celebrated village life, but he also included symbolic warnings against human folly of many kinds. The bagpipes in *Dragon Feathers* that are part animal are also reminiscent of Bosch's images of lurid creatures with musical horns. The oversized tray of food in the middle of the scene is right in front of the church roof in the distance; it is similar to symbolic tables or trays of food in paintings by Bosch and Brueghel, such as Brueghel's *The Land of Cockaigne* (1567), an allegory of gluttony and laziness (see Figure 7.3).

The bizarre combination of human and mythological creatures dancing, eating and drinking at Henry's wedding seems to suggest that the traditional happy ending for a folk hero and his bride never tells the whole story of magical transformation or human desires. The Dugins' pictorial narratives dramatizing the social and natural/ supernatural setting reveals the complex, inextricable links between good and evil that usually lie farther beneath the surface of the fairy tale narrative. Andrej Dugin explains that 'it is possible to say something unusual about common things and, conversely, to show the usual of the miracle. For me a plot serves as a ground for creating my own parallel visual stories. Without destroying a plot I try to show that it has many meanings' (Dugin, 1994).

It is particularly fascinating that the Dugins chose the years before and after 1500 in Northern European art as their primary inspiration for retelling this folk tale. They even placed the numerals 1510 around the monogram that looks like Dürer's, and the number 1500 appears on a farmhouse wall (the same date that is displayed prominently on Dürer's most famous self-portrait, in which he appears as a Christ-like figure). By 1500, artists from Jan Van Eyck onwards had been showing for more than half a century what they could achieve with oil paints, creating realistic and intricate detail on their canvases, while Dürer and others also worked with advances in printmaking. As we begin the 21st-century, we have enjoyed half a century of developments in technology that make colour reproductions of lavish paintings in picture books like this one widely available. In the transition from medieval to Renaissance art and thought, most art forms still depicted narratives – primarily Bible stories and sacred legends full of miraculous events. Some used continuous narrative, which occurs in several scenes in *Dragon Feathers* as Henry moves from left to right through his quest in each scene. In the illustrations containing continuous narrative and quatrefoil insets, these adaptations of medieval and Renaissance design elements make the narrative more real and dramatic, because we can see more of the action in one illustration. Yet at the same time they draw attention to the artificiality and magic of artistic representation, because we see Henry more than once in the same picture, or see inside and outside the farmer's house at the same time. The three monochrome quatrefoil insets, especially the one in which Henry's upper body in full colour reaches into the drab interior of the farmhouse, depict the magical solutions he brings back from the dragon as he returns gradually to realistic rural settings. *Dragon Feathers* demonstrates explicitly that the modern picture book is descended from illuminated manuscripts and also series of pictorial narratives produced by medieval and Renaissance artists as architectural ornamentations, wood-cuts, and engravings.

In their storytelling pictures at the dawn of the Protestant Reformation, Northern European artists were humanizing the sacred and giving domestic life a new level of respect and dignity. They continued to use familiar medieval symbols associated with traditional narratives, but they integrated biblical characters into settings full of

Happiest of all was Lucy when she saw her dear Henry again. She gazed into her beloved's eyes as he told her his story, then took him by the hand to see her father. Henry gave the innkeeper the three golden feathers, and since the woodcutter's son was now far richer than he himself, Lucy's father agreed to their marriage.

"Where in the world did you get all this money?" asked the innkeeper.

"From the dragon in the dark forest," replied Henry. "The easiest way to get there is to take the ferry."

The innkeeper set out at once, but strange to say, he was never heard from again.

Henry and Lucy invited all the people of the village to their wedding party in the courtyard of the inn. Everyone feasted and danced, but the young lovers danced longest into the night.

realistic details from nature and the folklife of their own culture, as 15th-century Europeans looked for clues in the visible world to the mysterious connections among everyday life, the trickery of the devil and the miracles of sacred history. People still believed that the natural and the supernatural co-existed all around them daily, a point of view preserved in the narratives of folk tales like *Dragon Feathers* when peasant heroes encounter magical forces. The phenomenon we call intertextuality was taken for granted in older traditions of storytelling and art. Medieval and Renaissance artists borrowed motifs and symbols from each other and copied each other's work, as storytellers have always done. Throughout the 20th-century, extensive study of folk tales showed us the ways they evolve and cross cultures. The complex art of a picture book like *Dragon Feathers* reflects our contemporary international awareness that beneath the seemingly simple narrative surfaces of the tales are subtexts with infinite depths of psychological and cultural significance.

I was attracted to *Dragon Feathers* because, in an extensive study of dragons in picture books, I found that a preponderance of recent books satirize old dragon tales or focus on the domestication or trivialization of tame and timid dragons, depicting dragons as comical and pathetic cartoon characters. On the other hand, some of the most talented storytellers and illustrators working today are reinvigorating the magic and mystery of ancient folklore in the pages of high quality books such as *Dragon Feathers*. They take folk tales and fairy tales seriously without abandoning humour or fun, elevating the status of folk literature and children's literature by creating picture books that are masterpieces of fine art. Their books help dispel the assumptions so prevalent in recent decades that picture books are only for the youngest children and beginning readers, that picture books this complex are not accessible or interesting to young children, and that artistically sophisticated illustrations too often detract from the verbal narrative or the reading process. As recent scholars such as Nodelman (1988), Doonan (1993) and Stewig (1995) have argued, children of all ages benefit in many ways from learning how to interpret the styles and codes of visual texts as well as verbal texts. According to Nodelman (1988), 'Good picture books offer us what all good art offers us: greater consciousness – the opportunity, in other words, to be more human. That means to be less innocent, more wise. It also means to feel more objectively and to think with more involvement' (1988).

Whenever I open *Dragon Feathers* in front of other people, friends and strangers of all ages are attracted by its fantastic art. The power of such books stems from the innovative ways they adapt older styles to contemporary retellings of traditional literature for children with pictorial narratives that, at different stages of study or individual development, may be enjoyed for their beauty and imagination, admired for their realistic details, or analysed in depth by older readers intrigued by the layers of literary and artistic intertextuality. As Teya Rosenberg (1998) has observed, the aesthetic enrichment gained from picture books that allude to particular styles from art history can work either way, starting with the picture books or reading them with previous knowledge of their sources. I have found that quite young children are captivated in their own way by the fantasy images throughout *Dragon Feathers*. My nephews pointed out details I had overlooked. Illustrator Paul Zelinsky (1998) notes that children first respond instinctively to the forms of art in ways that are difficult to explain. In a public library a child of about five, who had never seen me before, was drawn to *Dragon Feathers*, looked through it with me instead of exploring the hundreds of other children's books around her, and wanted to take it home. When I asked what she thought of the strange creatures on the endpapers, she said immediately that one was 'a fish-pipe.' Her matter-of-fact reaction to the blend of realism and fantasy images in this book reminded me that it is often adults, not young children, who are limited or inhibited in their responses. Sharing richly illustrated books with children allows us to learn from them as we help them become acquainted with the fascinating threads of the verbal and pictorial narratives woven together in different styles and colours within the intricate tapestries of world art and literature.

REFERENCES

Craft, R. (1975) *Pieter Brueghel's The Fair*. London: Collins.

Doonan, J. (1993) *Looking at Pictures in Picture Books*. Stroud, Glos.: Thimble Press.

Dugin, A. (1994) In *Something about the Author*, Vol. 77, pp. 60–61. Detroit: Gale.

Dugin, A. and Dugina, O. (1993) *Dragon Feathers*. Charlottesville, VA: Thomasson-Grant.

Esterl, A. (1991) *The Fine Round Cake*. Trans. P. Hejl. Illustrated by A. Dugin and O. Dugina. New York: Macmillan.

Garrett, J. (1996). Introduction. In B. Preiss (ed.) *The Best Children's Books in the World: A Treasury of Illustrated Stories*, pp. 7–9. New York: Abrams.

Gilman, P. (1984) *The Balloon Tree*. Richmond Hill, Ontario: North Winds.

MacGill-Callahan, S. (1993) *The Children of Lir*. Illustrated by G. Spirin. New York: Dial.

Mestrovic, M. (22 February 1991) 'Perestroika and picture books'. *Publishers Weekly*, 238, 128–31.

Nodelman, P. (1988) *Words about Pictures: The Narrative Art of Children's Picture Books*. Athens: University of Georgia Press.

Paley, N. (1991) 'Experiments in picture book design: modern artists who made books for children 1900–1985'. *Children's Literature Association Quarterly*, 16, 264–9.

Rackham, A. (1918) *English Fairy Tales*. Retold by F. A. Steel. New York: Macmillan, 1979.

Rosenberg, Teya (2 July 1998) 'The inspirations and resonances of art and art history in *Pish Posh, Said Hieronymus Bosch* and *When Cats Dream*'. Panel on the muse and the medium: painting, music, and dance in picture books. Children's Literature Association Conference, Paris.

Russell, F. (1967) *The World of Dürer, 1471–1528*. New York: Time-Life.

San Souci, R. (1990) *The White Cat*. Illustrated by G. Spirin. New York: Orchard.

Sanderson, R. (1993) *The Nativity*. Boston: Little, Brown.

Solomon, A. (10 November 1991) 'Those sumptuous Russian-flavored storybooks'. *New York Times Book Review*, 49.

Stanley, D. (1996) *Leonardo da Vinci*. New York: Morrow.

Stechow, W. (1990) *Pieter Bruegel the Elder*. New York: Abrams.

Stewig, J. W. (1995) *Looking at Picture Books*. Fort Atkinson, Wisconsin: Highsmith.

Willard, N. (1991) *Pish, Posh, Said Hieronymous Bosch*. Illustrated by D. Dillon and L. Dillon. San Diego: Harcourt Brace.

— (1981) *A Visit to William Blake's Inn*. Illustrated by M. Provenson and A. Provenson. San Diego: Harcourt Brace.

Yolen, J. (ed.) (1986) *Favorite Folk Tales from Around the World*. New York: Pantheon.

Zelinsky, P. O. (1998) Caldecott Medal acceptance. *Horn Book*, 74, 433–41.

— (1997) *Rapunzel*. New York: Dutton.

ARTWORKS

Bosch, H. (*c.* 1500) *Triptych of the Temptation of Saint Anthony*. Lisbon: Museu Nacional de Arte Antiga.

Brueghel, P. the Elder (1558) *The Alchemist*. Berlin: Kupferstichkabinett, Staatliche Museen.

— (1567) *Land of Cockaigne*. Munich: Alte Pinakothek.

— (1559) *Netherlandish Proverbs*. Berlin: Staatliche Museen.

— (1568) *The Peasants' Wedding*. Vienna: Kunsthistorisches Museum.

— (1566) *The Wedding Dance*. Detroit, Michigan: Institute of Arts.

Campin, R. (Master of Flémalle) (*c.* 1425–8) *The Merode Altarpiece*. New York: Metropolitan Museum of Art.

Cranach, L. (1510–12) *The Holy Kinship*. Vienna: Academie der Bildenden Künste.

da Messina, Antonella (1460) *St Jerome in his Study*. London: National Gallery.

da Vinci, L. (*c.* 1485) *The Virgin of the Rocks*. Paris: Musée du Louvre.

Dürer, A. (1513) *Knight, Death and Devil*. Cambridge, Massachusetts: The Fogg Museum of Art.

— (*c.* 1496) *The Prodigal Son*. Cambridge, Massachusetts: The Fogg Museum of Art.

— (1493) *Self-Portrait*. Paris: Musée du Louvre.

— (1500) *Self-Portrait*. Munich: Alte Pinakothek.

Grünewald, Matthias. (*c.* 1510–15) *The Isenheim Altarpiece* (*Crucifixion* on centre panel closed). Colmar, France: Musée d'Unterlinden.

Van Eyck, Jan (1434) *Arnolfini Double Portrait*. London: National Gallery.

Chapter 8

Tell Me a Picture: Stories in Museums

Frances Sword

The Fitzwilliam Museum is graceful, formal, peaceful and filled with works of art of extraordinary beauty. It is a university museum and as such has an air of scholarship. It is not perhaps a place one immediately links with children, but for the past ten years it has been my job – and my pleasure – to build an education service here. At first this seemed a daunting task, for at that time I held a set of preconceptions that warned me against matching children to this environment. Those preconceptions have long since been shattered and I have learnt that 'Beauty is a by-product of interest and pleasure in a choice of action' (Bronowski, 1978).

Although our choice of physical action is limited – the museum has no education space and everything must take place in the public galleries – interest is not; even if this situation imposes obvious restrictions, far more importantly it also creates an insurance of direct and continuous contact with the collections. The museum presents its wonderful art collections in an atmosphere of intense calm and this is my springboard, for the coiled energy within these works creates a contained world of potential interaction.

Those of us who teach in museums are privileged: we work with children who are temporarily freed from the tramlines of compulsion, we work largely outside direct curriculum constraints, we bring a fresh personality and a new environment to children, but above all we work with objects. Objects which, be they a painting by Pissarro or a steam engine, contain vital, potent ideas: time, death, belief, status, change and magic. Concepts such as these, visions, discoveries and beliefs are made concrete in the artefacts with which we teach.

The functions of many such objects are multifaceted and complex. An Egyptian coffin held more than a body, it held a belief system: the body was contained in the coffin, and the belief system was encapsulated and communicated through a deliberate and unique visual style. Many sorts of information are wrapped within this object, but, as is so often the case, style is the thickest and most complex cable of communication and presents the fundamental challenge of teaching through the visual arts. If language is taken to be 'the intentional conveyance of ideas from one living being to another through the instrumentality of arbitrary tokens or symbols agreed upon or understood by both as being associated with the particular ideas in question' (Butler, 1962), then dance and ceremony, music and physics, mathematics and painting can all be seen to operate as non-transferable languages. Visual styles are specific to time and place, they consist of elements of a visual language which communicates within the boundaries of cultural traditions. All languages can contain both simple and complex ideas, from $2+2 = 4$ to $E = mc^2$, from 'Ba Ba Black Sheep' to *The Marriage of Figaro*, and the span of the visual language is as wide as any other; within it an engineer's diagram bears a similar relation to a Rembrandt painting, as a written instruction leaflet does to a Shakespeare sonnet. Whatever the object, if it communicates through a visual style, we are presented with ideas held in line, shape, form and colour, ideas which are often more important and more complex than those held by any other aspects of the artefact.

Ideas held and communicated through visual language are presented to us simultaneously. Hence a map or diagram is often far more use than a list of spoken or written instructions that are passed on in serial form. This property of images, which lies at the heart of their power, can also create insecurities for viewers, for there is no built-in timescale to looking, there is no beginning or end as there is to a piece of music, a dance, a play or a book. Only our attention creates the start and finish. We can help children reach the riches of thought contained in visual form in many ways, most of which fundamentally depend on the creative use of words.

For many museum educators, discussion is the main teaching tool. With words we paint, mine, weave, pot and carve; we create environments and ceremonies; our words have to remake experiences to enable children to make sense of what they see. As an Egyptian coffin or a Holbein portrait holds information of many types, from simple material facts to tangled webs of belief and power, from construction techniques to the hopes and prayers of people long deceased, so we must try to express these complex ideas and help the object speak of every aspect of itself. In our efforts to introduce children to the abstract qualities encapsulated by material objects, the expression of our ideas through our choice of words begins to hold the same type of relationship to their purpose, as the style of an object bears to its function. Children and adults have often told me that having talked through a painting the image actually looks different. How we speak with children, the words we choose to carry meaning, have a profound effect on their capacity to observe, deduce and imagine.

This relationship between content and style in teaching, between ideas at the core and words that deliver can, I believe, be a key to unlock a child's imaginative contact with an object. The process begins with a selection of objects, and continues with a careful selection of ideas which must be communicated with an equally careful choice of words. Our words and phrasing are an enabling element of children's thinking. Our questions, which direct attention, create focus and open discussion, deserve close scrutiny.

In museums written information is usually delivered to the public as statements. It is rare to find a text that invites contribution or participation. In order to encourage children to observe, think and become involved, we ask them questions. Different types of questions can lead to various degrees of connection. Questions like 'How many colours can you see on the coffin?' and 'How are the planks joined together?' demand specific answers based on particular observations. These questions and the observations they stimulate are essential and form the basis of our work. But they can only reach so far. Observation should not be our final goal: I believe that for children to make their own connections to ideas encapsulated in visual form, we must move onwards from observation to deduction and imagination. We have an opportunity to do far more than direct attention to material detail. If we are to help children encounter the abstract realities held within visual style, we must use words in many ways. Questions can reach beyond the visible and bring children into a new relationship with objects:

'Is the coffin full of time?'
'Is time a solid, a liquid or a gas?'
'What do you think a soul is made of?'
'Where is my soul now?'

Questions like these play with concepts which formed the coffin just as surely as did the shape of an ancient adze. They enhance the capacity to observe and to learn by bringing a child into contact with the mystery of these objects – the meeting place of the physical and the metaphysical.

One day I sat in an exhibition of Holbein drawings, talking to a group of children with learning disabilities; one of them whose name was Catherine was 14 years old and very enthusiastic about the story of Henry VIII and his wives, three of whom were also her namesakes. A little later we all played a game which involved the children in finding similarities between drawings – everyone except Catherine that is, who stood gazing at one particular image of an unknown woman. I asked why she was looking at this drawing. Her answer took me completely by surprise. 'She loves me,' said Catherine, 'you can see it in her eyes.'

There are significant moments in every teacher's career, and this was one such moment for me. Catherine had cut through; she had related personally, strongly and confidently to the drawing. But how much had my teaching had to do with it? What was the relationship between Catherine, the unknown 16th-century woman, Holbein and me? The artist, the sitter and Catherine had formed a triangle. In what way had my talking affected Catherine's powers of imagination? Catherine had lifted off, she had made the moment her own, she had taken over. This is my aim for every child and for every group. Often this moment of lift-off is the moment a narrative is born.

There are layers of narratives in all museums. Each object is a vessel of its own history: it holds stories of makers and owners, discoverers and collectors. If an object is personified and its history seen as a lifespan, then we might say that as a baby it was raw material, as a child it was being formed, its adulthood was during its useful life and, finally, its existence in the museum can be thought of as an afterlife. This structure is useful in helping children contact the whole reality of an object; it helps them move beyond the museum and places them in the contrasting environments through which an object has travelled. It helps them meet the extraordinary variety of people who have had contact with the story of an object. These hidden people, the gatherers of materials, makers, owners, discoverers and collectors are still present, but need our help to speak of their stories. I have often found that their hands, the hands that made, held and used an object, now no longer touched, can bring a child into imaginative contact with a surface they can only encounter with their eyes.

Then there are the stories which are illustrated, told through paintings on carvings and reliefs, on objects and in pictures, tales told in wood and clay, paint and metal.

These stories can bring in their wake complexities of influence and association. When a group of nine-year-olds are seated in front of a 15th-century Italian Renaissance narrative painting that tells the story of Cupid and Psyche, they are seeing an object made in one country and one era whilst hearing a story from quite another; furthermore, the painting itself now hangs in a Victorian building fashioned after a Greek temple. The visual and physical environment hands down story and myth just as surely as any oral or written tradition. It absorbs adaptation and changes according to contemporary needs, just as all storytellers do.

There are stories linked to the museum environment by association, the galleries becoming a stage set with the vital and powerful evocation provided by real props. A Greek myth told among ancient Greek vases or the Mystery plays acted with Nativity paintings as scenery absorb new life, whilst the stories themselves invite a new interaction with the objects. Storytelling in a museum environment can shift the focus from the teller to the objects so the statues of Greek gods tell their own dramas and their forms make new meaning.

Then there are our own stories, those that we bring to the objects, our personal experiences that help us relate to them and to their time and place, 'My grandad was in Egypt in the war and he told me that ... ' All these types of stories are there for the telling, stories that exist as museum objects do, before we come on the scene. But museums offer more than an opportunity to tell stories; objects contain a potential that reaches beyond stories of themselves. They are a well of imaginative energy into which children can dip and become story-makers themselves.

A few years ago, I was working around the theme of water with a group of eight-year-olds; we were looking at a painting of a dark and stormy cove surrounded by high cliffs, a wrecked boat on the beach, and high on the cliffs, only just visible, a tiny group of people. We had talked at length about the weather, the time of year, the time of day, the size of the boat, the lay of the land, had the storm been and gone or was it just brewing? All these questions – and many more – could only be answered by direct observation. Then I asked if they could see any people in the painting. The people, once discovered, were the stimulus for much speculation about why they were on the cliff: were they rescuers or those who had been wrecked? were they signalling and if so to whom? was there a ship beyond the painting's edge? was there an island? was this an island? what sort of people were they? None of these were questions that could be answered by direct observation and so we had moved to deduction and speculation. Then I asked, 'If you were one of them, if you were stranded there, who would you like to have with you?' Without hesitation the children looked around at the paintings on the walls and chose two people from portraits on display (one of whom was George Bernard Shaw) to take as their companions. This was an extraordinary moment: the children had entered a painted world and needed to take painted people. They did not see these images as separate, each was linked to the next, a whole created through story.

This type of story-making has become an essential part of my work. It does not start with an invitation or an instruction, because 'let's make up a story' – or equivalent words – detaches the embryonic narrative, distinguishes it as a separate stage of what should be a continuous process. The moment of lift-off arrives when, saturated with information gathered from their own observations and deductions, the children's imaginative process meets that of the artist and the child becomes active, becomes a maker and in my opinion a learner. For 'to learn' is an active verb.

In my experience of working in museums, I have come to think of information as food for the child's imaginative process. Imagination, our personal manipulation of experience, depends on an acute and fierce relationship with the flimsy boundary between external and internal reality, the same border that is explored and made concrete in visual works of art. If, as is commonly accepted, the quality of an experience affects the nature of our response, then it follows that exposure to those objects that we categorize as art, objects which give form to the invisible, that make thoughts tangible, that show the thread that joins the objective to our subjective perceptions of a shared reality, will leave their mark – and they do. This is the fundamental value of teaching with works of art, the forging of connections, times and places, cultures and minds, linked through objects made to communicate.

The realization of how children make connections, how – to them – separate images or artefacts can form a holistic unit, gave me the confidence to try forming new links. Wherever objects are deliberately arranged, they are placed to achieve a particular purpose: instruments placed on a surgeon's trolley follow the essential order of an operation: objects in a shop window are arranged to focus attention and tempt us to buy. Museum objects are deliberately sorted and placed to communicate various types of information about time, place, materials, makers and context. But meaning is slippery. An apple by a fig leaf creates one meaning, an apple on a little boy's head tells a different story.

The placing of objects in museums usually follows traditional patterns of scholarship augmented by aesthetic considerations. Educators working in museums often need to cut through these traditional arrangements and create patterns to meet their own needs. If, for example, the reason for a visit is to work around the theme of wood – a clearly defined idea, but one that could demand the use of widely spaced objects – a current of concentration has to be created, the session has to build and form a shape, rather than be a series of disconnected information points. There are many ways to focus children's attention but it is hard to create a natural flow of information that moves from one object to the next. A narrative stream formed around the objects creates a context for the flow of information and helps children recall the objects, their observations and the information held in a story. In this way, returning to the theme of wood, a simple story woven together with the children might start with their observations of 17th-century Dutch genre paintings. From these we might select an apprentice, our central character whom we would name. We would select information from the paintings to build a picture of his life, use landscape paintings to gather information about trees available in the Netherlands, and paintings of ships to stimulate thinking about trade. Using a sequence of pieces of furniture, I could help the children observe construction techniques and the skills needed to become a master cabinet-maker. We might end with the apprentice's masterpiece. The purpose of a storyline is always to construct an energetic framework which encourages, through a dramatic and increasing flow of interest, intense observation and visual interaction.

I do not use this method of teaching lightly for it brings important questions into sharp focus. Creating a narrative framework around researched objects puts the educator on the line between fact and fiction, between story and history; for the process utilizes clear, specific, authenticated facts about objects, but also reaches into an indistinct hinterland of information. For example, it may be known that a pot was made by a named potter who worked in a particular pottery at a specific time. It may have been discovered by a known individual and collected by another, all this is clear and authenticated. However, it is also self-evident that the clay had to be dug and cleaned, the kiln fuelled and fired, the pot sold and used. All the people involved in these processes were as important as the potter, but they have become anonymous and this is the information hinterland. The question is then posed, should we only talk about named people and authenticated facts, or can we give those who have become anonymous their due presence through story? This question demands that we also examine issues of class, for the anonymous players in these stories of objects often belonged to less privileged sections of society who can all too easily be forgotten. I therefore question the validity of only presenting facts that can be verified, for then we are in danger of painting a picture that leaves such gaps that it can actually misrepresent the culture from which the object springs.

The use of narrative as a supportive context for factual content has long since been used in children's history books and, to the best of my knowledge, this mode of presentation goes unquestioned. We are all familiar with history books which present factual information through fictional characters; texts such as *Patronius Visits the Forum* pass without comment, but who was Patronius, and did he visit the Forum? I suggest that just as we accept the blend of known facts about the Forum and the fictional character who brings it to life in a written form, so should we in the oral tradition and in a museum setting.

Taking a longer perspective, the very purpose of story is in its essence informative, the form of the story and the style of its delivery creating a particular meaning. Once created a story has its own time and rhythm, its own pace and emphasis which in turn becomes shaped in the mind of the listener. I once sat riveted to a film of an Amazonian Indian father teaching his small son how to look after his new baby brother. The boy had left the baby unguarded on the ground and so the father told him and a group of village children a story about a baby monkey that was stolen away because its mother left it at the bottom of a tree. He repeated his story three times until the children recited it with him. He did not need to make any explicit reference to the baby brother. The story did all the necessary teaching.

I am firmly convinced of the power of story as a tool for learning, a stimulus for observation and as a place where the creative thinking of an artist can meet the creative energy of children. In a museum setting the use of story does not need to challenge historical accuracy, but it can question the relationship between facts and the style in which they are delivered. Working within the framework of story-making in an art museum, I have come to realize that I am grappling with topics which lie at the heart of this environment. For the relationship between fact and interpretative context creates a fundamental tension and is a central focus of current discussion in the area of museum display. The creative use of words within a museum setting is another facet of this debate. Perhaps it is this very tension that makes story such a powerful medium in art museums or perhaps it's just that one good art form deserves another.

REFERENCES

Bronowski, Jacob (1978) *The Visionary Eye*. London: MIT Press.
Butler, Samuel (1962) *The Importance of Language*, Max Black (ed.). New York: Spectrum.

Chapter 9

'Beware Beware': Image, Word and Apprehension

Jane Doonan

> Landscapes are culture before they are nature; constructs of the imagination projected
> onto wood and water and rock . . . For although we are accustomed to separate nature and
> human perception into two realms, they are in fact, indivisible. Before it can ever be a
> response for the senses, landscape is the work of the mind. Its scenery is built up as much
> from strata of memory as from layers of rock.
>
> Simon Schama, *Landscape and Memory*

Beware Beware, written by Susan Hill and illustrated by Angela Barrett, is a picture book with a text of innovative narrative structure, and artwork which displays intensity of imagination. The story might well be described as one in which very little happens, but the multi-modal discourse is such a skilful creation of ambiguity that it can support two major themes. One is about the struggle to balance the needs of dependence and claims of independence in an early stage of a child's development. The other is the idea that cognition and culture determine our apprehension of the real world. Hill and Barrett communicate these concepts so successfully that children from about seven years old with whom I have shared *'Beware Beware'* readily recognize the truth-to-experience which the picture book presents. How does it do it? The intention of this chapter is to consider some of the ways in which the words, images and the material object itself, effect the temporal-spatial construction of story and significance – bring it into being. The discussion below will focus upon narrative and pictorialization processes and designs, including point of view, focalization and perspectival shifts, layout and framing; the function of the primary motif, a wood, and the visual motif, a window, in the development of the themes; intertextuality.

   The story content follows a traditional pattern, with the title and setting standing in relationship with the folktale genre. In a cottage close by a wood live a mother and her daughter of about seven years old. Late one winter's afternoon, whilst her mother is busy baking, the child slips away by herself to explore the wood. Once there she becomes increasingly frightened, and turns back. Meanwhile her mother comes to look for her. They are reunited and go home.

   Conflict is an important element of the plot. The child acts against her mother's wishes, a person-to-person conflict which a young audience readily understands from firsthand experience. She is in psychological conflict with herself. The story also presents an ideological conflict; as a society we see individuality and enterprise as desirable traits in children, whilst putting an equally strong value on parental wisdom and authority. There are three physical locations: the home, restrictive but safe, the wood, representing freedom but danger, and the snowy field which lies between.

The theme concerned with balancing the needs of dependence and the claims of independence takes the form of a quest to discover 'what's out there' but it is also the inner quest that all young children undertake as a test of their strength when they feel ready to relinquish their infantile dependency wishes. For the symbolic pictorialization of this theme Barrett selects a window as the major recurring motif, an object which is not named in the text, and uses it with great skill, both as a mimetic and an expressive image. There are no fewer than six scenes showing the same window in *Beware Beware*, but through changes in viewpoint, context and stage of story, the significance changes.

ON THE THRESHOLD

The image of the window, at close distance, appears on the front cover. The view from the window gives on to a snowy field, heavily shadowed where it meets the edges of a wood. Before the window stand mother and child, in profile, looking at each other. The mother clasps the little girl's hands within her own. What is the nature of the exchange between them? We are drawn into speculation through that look – the way the figures are posed. In this case the mother appears to be giving a warning, extracting or giving a promise. 'Promise me that you won't go off on your own . . . ', or maybe she is saying, 'I promise that we'll go there soon'. We cannot be sure, but in close proximity to their joined hands and just sticking out of the mother's apron pocket is the top of a measuring spoon with a broken string through the hole in the handle. This small detail perhaps is alluding to the fact that promises, like things, get broken.

The portrayal of the mother, a pre-Raphaelite figure, includes an interpretative puzzle because it has a Janus-like aspect. She turns a radiant and loving face towards the child, but in the nape of her neck, the coils of her abundant hair form another face with an anguished or fearsome expression, pointing in the opposite direction. Does this image symbolize the mother's fears for her daughter in relation to exploring the wood, or does it exemplify a negative aspect of motherhood? As for the window with its strong vertical and horizontal emphases created by the glazing bars, it provides an effective barrier between the outside world and the interior, the unknown and the known.

Susan Hill's poetic, verbal narrative shapes both main themes by its own structure. Description alternating with non-narrated representation moves the reader between exterior and interior spaces. The discourse is anchored to the contemporary time of the action. Here are the opening lines (see also Figure 9.1):

Kitchen's warm.
Smells of spice.
Kettle sings.
Fire bright.
But what's out there?
Beware, beware.

Kitchen's warm.

Smells of spice.

Kettle sings.

Fire bright.

But what's out there?

Beware, beware.

Figure 9.1

To make meanings the reader is required to fill gaps, to make inferences, not only between sentences, but between the lines. And how is the text to be performed? Descriptive statements ranging from a single line to five-line sequence indicate a covert narrator acting as a voiceover for the scene being shown. These passages refer to material reality – mainly the landscape of the story. Interspersed with the description are repetitions of the words of the title which acquire exclamation marks as the tension rises – too strongly expressive to belong to a covert narrator. Perhaps this refrain is the mother's, telling her child to be careful; or at these points does the narrator give way to a dramatic chorus of whisperers, a mysterious source, directly warning? To give some idea of the increasing emphasis and the subsequent effect upon the rhythms of the narration, the refrain will be quoted at appropriate points in this chapter.

Inner reality – the mindscape – is represented by non-mediated narrative, recording the child's and the mother's thoughts, or possibly words. There are no speech marks to indicate which but interior monologue seems most likely. Certainly the language of some of the lines is identifiably that of the child, thinking about her present experience; other lines might be alluding to previous conversations held with her mother and now recalled in snatches, in which case the past inhabits the present. There is no presumptive audience other than the thinker herself, and no deference to the interpretative needs of a narratee. One cannot be sure what attitudes are being implied. Within the narrative these lines can function as 'strata of memory' (a phrase I am borrowing from Simon Schama, because I cannot better it). As one reads them one constructs a mental image of what lies beneath the verbal surface – 'seeing' the exchanges between mother and child though one cannot quite picture them as one does real images, because mental images are not exclusively visual. The descriptive statements and interior monologue(s) stand in relationship with each other and all performance choices will affect the nature of the relationship between the words and the images. The narrative processes of *Beware Beware* are such that a picture book is the only possible medium for this particular story – it could not be adapted for other media such as film or television with a soundtrack, without destroying the most important of the creative gaps which the reader has to fill: deciding how to tell the story.

Before moving on to an analysis of the picture which accompanies the opening of the verbal narrative, and which includes the second image of the window, the functions of frames, framing and layout have to be considered. Frames (the external boundaries enclosing the picture itself) and designs in layout in picture books play a functional part in visual communication. They act like pauses, disconnecting one picture from another or from adjacent text. Just as pauses in conversation or in movement may be brief or prolonged, carry varying significance, so 'visual framing, too, is a matter of degree; elements of the composition may be strongly or weakly framed' (Kress and Leeuwen, 1996). The layout for *Beware Beware* is designed in double-page compositions with superimposed text thus integrating word and image. These compositions are framed by the cut edge of the paper on all four sides. This is the lightest, least assertive way of framing a picture, minimizing the boundaries between the pictorial world and the real one. But framing also occurs within individual pictures, by discontinuities of colour or shape or simply an empty space between the elements. The internal framing affects the perceptual weight, emphasis and psychological value likely to be given to the perceived images and this is particularly evident in the opening double spread of *Beware Beware*.

The picture which accompanies the text (quoted above) is designed in three episodes, internally framed, each containing a figure, or metonymic symbols for figures. The effect encourages the audience to move slowly over the picture plane taking in each episode from a slightly different viewpoint and thereby gaining an overview. The conflict of interests between mother and child is expressed through the structure of the composition.

In the first episode to the left, the mother is preparing food, the cat sleeps. They are framed by blue vertical emphases which denote the left side of the chimney breast, and the interior partitions which form a small entrance hall. The view from the window in mother's part of the kitchen is of a protective hedge and sun on snow.

The kitchen table top, seen from an oblique angle, is framed by flagstones. Mother's cooking utensils, biscuit dough and a cut-out gingerbread man at one end of the table are anchored in the middle lower foreground, and further down the table lie the child's playthings – a spinning top, doll and story book. Though relatively small in scale, the latter objects are given perceptual weight by their position on the picture plane, to the lower right corner, where they are 'pulling away' as if drawn by magnets. The table displays contrasting symbols of nourishment for the body and stimulation for the mind, of the duties of parenthood and the unburdened hours of childhood.

In the third episode, the child is looking at the snowy field and shadowed wood, through the window already shown on the cover. Strongly framed to the left by the porch partition and a wooden chair, she is cut off from her mother, the source of warmth, and the cat. She is seen from behind. The relation of her figure and the landscape bears a privacy and an intensity. The child is posed like a figure from a Northern Romantic painting by Caspar David Friedrich, *Woman at a Window* (1822), with the window having 'the significance of the eye in a body – which is the house, and from which one observes and experiences the world' (Hammacher, 1986). The window is a threshold. In the history of painting, the image of the window-as-threshold covers a span of nearly two hundred years; the window which opens into space and into life outside has played this role since Friedrich, up to Matisse, and was restored by Magritte who makes us aware of indoor and outdoor spaces which meet in his paintings to which I refer below. The function of the window-as-threshold in the first story opening of *Beware Beware* develops the theme which is introduced on the cover, as well as providing the opportunity for intertextual interplay for adults, and for those children who may subsequently encounter examples in fine art and remember Barrett's picture.

On the second opening, Barrett moves her viewer outside the house, and taking the convention of the window-as-threshold, she uses it in a highly original way (see Figure 9.2).

Setting sun
Rose red.
Light falls
Across the snow.
Path winds.

Setting sun

Rose red.

Light falls

Across the snow.

Path winds.

Who's to know?

Don't go!

But what's out there?

Figure 9.2

Who's to know?
Don't go!
But what's out there?

Who speaks? A narrator, and the voices of conscience, commonsense, and curiosity perhaps. Moving to the picture, knowing a little about how perspective works helps to find an answer to the question, Who sees? The most important function of a perspective is to establish the position of the viewer in relation to the picture; by the position in which the artist establishes herself, and also therefore the viewer, the artist states an attitude to the image which she is making. The viewpoint establishes the point of view – perceptual and attitudinal.

Two different subject positions have been designed for the viewer to hold but this composition is so complex that one of the two positions affords an additional variant: the most obvious position places the viewer, as an observer, outside the window, close-up, opposite the child. Since a picture is virtual reality, one cannot see one's own reflection upon the glass as would be the case in reality; but the absence makes the pictorial effect all the more haunting. Or the viewer may switch between this position and the others which Barrett has constructed, so that one can be either inside looking out, or again, outside observing the front of the house but from a distance. The window glass makes this possible. Its reflection shows the view of the wood (which would lie behind the close-up observer), focalized or as seen by the child, which allows the viewer to share her perspective of the snowy landscape – a subjective experience.

The picture's horizontal angle is designed with the frontal plane of the artist (and hence the viewer) and the frontal plane of the image parallel, which allows for the maximum 'involvement' between the two. The picture content is open to us. The vertical angle is designed so that the child and the viewer meet at eye level, which will be necessary if the illusion that we are looking through her eyes is to be sustainable. The three dimensional space is constructed in a series of receding planes. The picture plane is denoted by the wall and the foremost edge of the glazing bars. Just behind lie the window panes, with the child's form and the jug on the other side of the glass. This is shallow depth. The middle and far planes belong to the interior of the room but visibility becomes compromised and confused by the scene which the panes reflect from outside the front of the house. The glass is both transparent and reflective. The viewer observes phantom shapes of the table, bowl and chair back, and overlying these, stronger details of the brightly lit reflected scene. The long shadow, in which the wood lies, now falls upon the girl. But once one's interest is taken by that view of the wood, the picture field doubles in depth, with implied space stretching in front of the house to the edge of the woods as well as from the front of the house to the back of the kitchen. Then the position of the child appears to shift from the near planes to a near-middle distance because the world in the picture is experienced as a direct continuation of the viewer's own space.

There are further complications: the child's figure may be interpreted as being inside looking out, but through the construction of the composition, and a detail like the placement of the jug, the observer-viewer feels that the child, a ghostly figure, might almost be outside looking in. The glazing bars keep her out, keep her in. As an abstract element, the bars isolate and frame her face and, in turn, the shape of the face isolates and frames the eyes.

The child gazes out of the window in the observer's line of vision. The gaze, as a pictorial device, has a long history going back to early Christian icons. A gaze from a represented participant to a viewer is the most powerful way an artist has of drawing the latter into the pictorial world – creating a position for that viewer which makes her or him an imaginary participant in the scene, taking up 'a pseudo-social bond' with the gazer, in much the same way as in real life when someone makes us the object of her or his direct look (Kress and Leeuwen, 1996). In Barrett's picture the object of the child's gaze is not the viewer, but the wood. One no longer know where one stands. The effect of the artist's use of the direct gaze imbues the wood with a spirit, a life-force: the power of the mother's injunctions are in the balance against the power of the wood in the child's animistic mind.

Barrett emphasizes the reflective action of the eyes, with highlights on the cornea. Jonathan Miller explains, 'although the reflected gleam is purely an optical phenomenon, it is consistently visualised as an expression of the personal vitality of the sitter, and an artist who wishes to convey the attentive liveliness of his subject is somehow obliged to reproduce the glint in the eye' (Miller, 1998). But Barrett makes marks which are more than a conventional dab of white on the iris. The rose red light on the snow is reflected, not only on the iris, but spreading over the pupil.

Nature is both dead and alive: dead in the bare branches, alive in its power to move like Birnam Wood. The plants outside appear as cracks in the 'reality' of the glass. The snowy landscape appears to have invaded the child's eyeballs. The child's finger presses against the glass, a contact point through which power flows in both directions. The window is not a shield to protect the child but a conductor.

The next three openings carry the child away from the house. In the first of these, the window is shown from a very oblique angle, of no practical significance for the child who is now *out there* on her way to the wood. *Beware, beware!*

IN THE LONG SHADOW

There is a long history in our culture associated with the wood and life being a journey of self-discovery. Dante's *selva oscura* has its roots in 'the ancient Roman idea of the dark wood as a place where one lost one's way' (Schama, 1995). The dark forests of folk and fairy tales are traditional settings for tests and adventures. This convention without the repeated incantation would prepare all but the youngest readers for the shape of the story. The artist reduces the scale of the child in stages, from the time when she slips out of the house. In the scene showing the child about to enter the wood the viewpoint is from overhead and within the trees: a bird's eye view. There is a foreboding atmosphere created by both word and image. The child stands looking back towards her home. She is framed in bare boughs and isolated in negative space, the size and colour of a fledgling, and just as vulnerable (see Figure 9.3).

The concept of landscape, built up as much from strata of memory as from layers of rock, now begins to be strongly expressed iconically, in partnership with the text. Barrett and Hill give picture book form to the notion expressed in the extract from Simon Schama's book at the head of this chapter. Barrett's use of the window motif also allows scope for interplay in relation to a painting by Magritte entitled, *La Condition Humaine*. Magritte's painting shows an open window with an easel in front of it; the

Birds cold

Branches bare

What's over there?

Not far.

I can look back

I'm taking care

I'm there! I'm there!

Figure 9.3

canvas on the easel bears a picture of the view through the window, and this picture exactly overlaps the view, so that the play between 'image' and 'reality' inside the fiction of Magritte's image asserts that the real world is merely a construction of the mind. In a 1938 lecture featuring the painting, Magritte argued that we see the world as being outside ourselves even though it is only a mental representation of what we experience on the inside. According to Simon Schama, Magritte means that, 'What lies beyond the window pane of our apprehension . . . needs a design before we can properly discern its form, let alone derive pleasure from its perception. And it is culture, convention, and cognition that makes that design: that invests a retinal impression with the quality we experience as beauty' (Schama, 1995). When we walk through unfamiliar territory – take a walk on the wild wood side – the design, together with our survival instincts, invest retinal impressions and sounds with qualities we associate with danger.

In the picture book the child imports memories of the tales she has been told or read, and from them she takes the forms for her fears. She enters the wood and the branches open to let her pass into the world of her imagination. Colour which has been used for naturalistic effect now gives way to hues and tones which signify the child's emotions. The physical format of the page also changes, so that the sequence within the wood opens and closes with split half-pages designed with a curvular or wavy edge; these have both perceptual and psychological functions. Looking at the pictures and turning the page, one is not really sure where things begin or end – boundaries are blurred. The wood is experienced as a period of indeterminate time in an unmappable place where inside and outside spaces and states of being meet and merge: indivisible.

Within the wood, initially the child is shown dwarfed by tree trunks upon which animal masks are materializing. *Beware! Beware!* A turn of the page and the scene is focalized by the child who is not represented, so one sees from the same vantage point as the child (in the language of film and television this is called the subjective camera). The 'window pane of our apprehension' takes on double meaning: understanding and dread. This subjective position is designed for the scene-viewer to occupy for three consecutive pictures and it is not until the child is out of the wood that she again becomes a represented participant. At first, in green and azure, with textures of gauze and moss come the Cottingley fairies and Shakespearean sprites, but also amongst them, staring eyes and goblin faces. The branches through which the child has entered the wood begin to close behind her.

Over the page opening, and to a pictorialization which shows fears spreading to the edges of the child's world; colour changes to brown-gray and drained pink; animal imagery threatens. A real wolf lurks half-concealed by a tree. A huge trunk rears up as a grizzly bear. A dragon swells to fill a far part of the forest floor. *Beware! Beware!* The next turn of the page brings the child and audience to the heart of the woods and the climax of the story (see Figure 9.4):

Crooked chimneys
Caves Ghosts
Trolls Elves
Weasels Stoats
Gingerbread house

Crooked chimneys

Caves Ghosts

Trolls Elves

Weasels Stoats

Gingerbread house

Giant's cave

Whistling laughter

Echoes.

Brave? No, no
back there
back there.

Figure 9.4

Giant's cave
Whistling laughter
Echoes.

The picture replicates the literary references of the text; the roots of the forest floor writhe as stoats and weasels, the picture field tunnels away into the far distance, lined by gibbering terrors constructed from the dark side of nursery rhyme, folk, fantasy and fairy tales. The setting undergoes a transformation as Barrett pictorializes the psychological fears within a physical framework; we are not just inside the girl's mind but as if inside her body, like a camera taking a trip along her internal passages. Traditionally the lungs are represented as the branches of trees, and in the picture the forest paths are like the cartilage rings of the girl's airways.

Brave? No, no
   back there
      back there.

The audience is restored to the natural world in the following opening. The mother, in medium close-up, is positioned on the left half of the picture plane, the wood lies on the right. Birds fly low above the snowy fields and in a flock above the far horizon. She is crossing the no-man's land, and anxiously scanning the wood. Within the fringes of the wood, very small in scale, the child is running between the trees, head down. The mother does not see the child, the child cannot see her mother. *Oh, **where?*** The split page on the recto, as it is turned, makes three distinctive contributions to the spatial-temporal construction of the drama. The split-page moves the child out of the wood to place her within her mother's arms and pictorial space. It implies the passage of time by a shift in the far flock of birds and the disappearance of the low-flying ones, and the appearance of a small rabbit which bobs up by the hedge. Thirdly, the split-page completes the change from fantasy to realism in the way the trees are represented. *Oh, there.*

DRAWING THE CURTAINS

Beware Beware concludes with the child safely home in the physical sense. But the discourse of both semiotic systems implies that this could be the end of only part of a story.

Kitchen's warm.
Smells of spice.
Curtains drawn.
Fire bright.
Night.
But ***what's*** out there?

The picture shows a kitchen scene. The setting mirrors the mood of the first five lines. At the table, the mother, in the left foreground, seated and in profile, pauses from her sewing to look reflectively at her daughter. The child, also seated, turns towards the window behind her, as if in response to something she is thinking, or hears, or possibly fears. This final depiction of the window shows the curtains drawn across, signifying protection, closing off the site of the quest. The leafy patterned fabric, which mimics the foliage of the forest, exemplifies the power of the forest tamed for domestic decorative purpose. We cannot see the child's face. In inferencing what she is feeling or why she has turned, do we to take our cue from the man's sock on the chair? Perhaps sounds of her father's return have reached her. Or do we make something different, from the appearance of the child's doll, beside her hand, which lies on its back, with an alarmed expression on its face. Near the door, the cat with its lifted paw and tail, indicates that either it wants to go outside, or it senses something disturbing. The cat stares in the girl's direction, alert. But what's out there? The words will not tell and the image does not show.

Can one argue for a closed ending? That is possible if we ascribe the final line of the text to the mother, expressing her thoughts for her child when she goes out into the world sometime in the future. Within the story-time the child's curiosity gets the better of her, but no immediate harm is done. Mother knows best, and what happened was lesson enough for the young transgressor: society approves such an outcome. If the child voices the final line, it may be taken as an indication that her curiosity is re-surfacing, though she may well be very happy to be safely within her home for the present.

Reviewing the significance of the whole, as the picture book covers close, leaves many ideas still in play. The ending is ambiguous if the audience remains a detached viewer of the scene, particularly the poses of child and cat. Perhaps the child has daydreamed the visit to the wood, never left the house and her curiosity is as powerful as ever. Alternatively, having left the safety of her home, perhaps the child becomes bewitched by the forces of the forest – she will go back – she is spellbound. Something is out there. The latter interpretation might be more disturbing to adults than to children, who as Inglis points out, ' ... like a dose of the horrors at times – well-controlled times, with a warm fire and all the lights on all the way upstairs to bed' (Inglis, 1981).

An intertextual visual allusion introduces another dimension. Mother is the owner of a long red hooded cloak which hangs on a peg by the door. Our last view of her shows her sewing, making something out of a large piece of soft, red cloth – a cloak for her daughter perhaps, to hang on the empty peg beside the other one? A broken promise, a wolf in the wood? Are we being invited to weigh the content of the picture book, our focused text, against that of the old folktale, the pre-text? If so, 'because of the coexistence within the one discourse space of a pre-text and focused text the significance of the story will tend to be situated not in the focused text but in the process of interaction between the text. That is, the effect is intertexual in its fullest sense' (Stephens, 1992).

In common with folk tales, the picture book also invites an interpretation applying a psychoanalytic model of the human personality, with the wood symbolizing the world of our unconscious. The id, colliding with the ego, and the promptings of the superego, set the stage for the inner conflict:

I'm here, out there.
Beware, beware!
I will take care.

The child's undeveloped personality cannot master her acute and natural anxieties, the most extreme being death, signalled by the wild creatures and the gingerbread house.

Another idea which remains in play is to return to the picture book, and consider the resonances of the phrase, *In long shadow lies the wood*, and see how much might be made from that, together with the shadow motif and the use of light and dark colour tones as structural elements, and colour symbolism generally throughout the sequence of pictures.

As indicated above, the picture book's rich potential for creative play is both a distinguishing feature and a strength. *Beware Beware* will sustain repeated readings and reward further explorations in feeling and thinking for children, as well as those whose interest lies in any of the many aspects of the picture book medium.

REFERENCES

Hammacher, A.M. (1986) *Magritte*. London: Thames and Hudson.

Hill, S., illustrated by Angela Barrett (1993) *Beware Beware*. Walker Books: London.

Inglis, F. (1981) *The Promise of Happiness*. Cambridge: Cambridge University Press.

Kress, G. and Van Leeuwen, T. (1996) *Reading Images: The Grammar of Visual Design*. London: Routledge.

Miller, J. (1998) *On Reflection*. London: National Gallery Publication.

Schama, S. (1995) *Landscape and Memory*. London: Harper Collins.

Stephens, J. (1992) *Language and Ideology in Children's Fiction*. London: Longman.

IV

Literary Narratives

Chapter 10

'Play Out the Play': Approaching Shakespeare's Plays with Primary School Children through Active Storytelling

Sarah Gordon

Active storytelling is a way of introducing children to Shakespeare by taking part in his stories. It is a practical approach which, as the phrase implies, is about doing, about firing a child's imagination and encouraging the child to participate in the living world of a story by being there. Through active storytelling children become involved in firsthand experience of the story, its characters, its language, its plot. They play out its complexities, its very life as it unfolds, becoming the storytellers who are discovering, enacting and telling the story.

I began to develop this active storytelling approach to Shakespeare through a school-based research degree in 1987 and have developed the methodology through theory and practice since that time. What began as a method of exploration and discovery in schools has become, in practice, a working strategy for opening up Shakespeare's stories as an extraordinary resource bank for children. Through the 1990s the active storytelling method has been integrated by many theatre companies who work with children, reflecting its dual roots in the spheres of education and performance. As we approach the millennium many primary school children, along with teachers and actors, will have breathed life into Shakespeare through active storytelling.

What follows is an in-depth look at active storytelling – how and why it works with Shakespeare's stories, the background to the work, the influences behind its development and, finally, practical strategies for approaching Shakespeare with primary school children.

THE HOW AND WHY

The experience of active storytelling is an extension of children's play and involves commitment and imaginative engagement from all participants. It is the process through which children become imaginatively and emotionally immersed in the world of Shakespeare's plays. Through active storytelling, the story, language and characters are interwoven in the creation of a unique fictional world, a world in which fantasy and reality blur and disbelief is willingly suspended. This world of the play has few boundaries or rules. It does not depend on historical or geographical accuracy. Children relate their own personal experiences to the world of the play; if children want to imagine that they are preparing 'jelly and ice-cream with nuts on top' for Macbeth's banquet then these ideas can be integrated into their developing imaginative worlds. For some children relevant historical study may broaden their understanding of the setting of the play, but, in active storytelling, the priority is enjoyment of the stories through imaginative involvement.

Part of the magic of exploring Shakespeare's plays through active storytelling revolves around the fact that children do not know the story first. Initially they do not even know it is Shakespeare. They gain access to the story, to the heart of the play itself, through prediction and discovery. They live through the story, discussing and predicting what might happen next by putting themselves in the shoes of the characters.

To enable children to 'play out the play' there is a central emphasis on the use of the in-role drama process. Through active storytelling children are encouraged to interpret – to make their own decisions about the story and to develop their own images of, and relationships with, the characters. A helpful strategy is to ask for volunteers to wear sticky labels showing the names of their characters. This helps children to differentiate between the characters in the story and, with some repetition, encourages them to use the characters' names, often their first point of access to the language of the play. The child wearing the label is not necessarily an 'actor'; in fact, as the story develops, many members of the group take on the voices and feelings of various characters. The 'labelled' child is not being put in the spotlight for anything other than identification purposes, although it is interesting to see how some children seize the opportunity to perform and immerse themselves completely in the role.

As children 'play out the play' they are involved as the characters and the storytellers in bringing the play to life. The text is never static; it is a working, ever-changing structure. Nor is the text a document, or even a written script, but a collaborative journey of discovery into a special fictional world. This journey, facilitated both by teacher and child, actively involves the participants in the stories and the language of the plays which become interwoven, as Shakespeare's language becomes a key point of access to the imaginative world the children are building up. Through repetition and familiarity, through using short accessible sections of the text, children come to possess the words as their own. Young children have an innate love of rhythm and rhyme; they enjoy speaking Shakespeare's words and exploring different ways of saying them.

Active storytelling is a participatory process, a positive, non-competitive approach, where all of the children are encouraged to be involved all of the time. Because the emphasis is on interpretation rather than right or wrong answers, all children, whatever their previous achievement, have the opportunity to succeed and to increase in confidence, allowing children of all abilities and social backgrounds to be active participants in the world of Shakespeare's plays.

INFLUENCES AND BACKGROUND

Prior to my research on Shakespeare in primary schools, I had some practical experience, although no wider evidence, of the appeal of Shakespeare's stories and language to young children. I was fired with enthusiasm by the response of 9 to 11-year-olds to

Macbeth, where it became apparent that the impact of Shakespeare on their learning and their lives was extraordinary. The Shakespeare and Schools Project, directed by Dr Rex Gibson, was especially influential. This large-scale research and development project, set up in 1986 at the Cambridge Institute of Education, revolutionized Shakespeare teaching across the country. Working as a participant in this project, I was inspired and encouraged by Dr Gibson's work. In particular, his commitment to introducing primary pupils to Shakespeare's plays, and his belief in the capacity of young children to possess Shakespeare's language, were major influences on my active storytelling methodology, where Shakespeare's language is the pivotal point of access for a child's imaginative involvement in the story and the play.

> Shakespeare is difficult but it never pays to underestimate the capacity of primary children. Their delight in new and demanding words, their love of rhythm, rhyme, structure, emphasis, sound itself; their intuitive and often uninhibited grasp of the physical aspects of language; all these are fulfilled by Shakespeare.
>
> (Gibson, 1987)

At the time of researching active approaches to Shakespeare in primary schools, two major reports appeared, both of which contributed to programmes of study for the English National Curriculum. Neither the Kingman Report (DES, 1988) on the Teaching of English Language, nor the Cox Report (DES, 1989), made any explicit reference to the place of Shakespeare's plays in the primary school curriculum, although the Cox Report included story versions of Shakespeare in its list of recommended reading.

Now things have changed – a little. In the National Literacy Strategy (DfEE, 1998) the study of a Shakespeare play is recommended in Year 6, term one and the general principles of active storytelling are in tune with it, in terms of aiming for a child's imaginative involvement in story and literature. However 'literacy hour' work is text-based and not drama-based. My fear is that, without an initial imaginative plunge into the very heart of the story itself, a text-based study alone could revert back to the days of traditional, academic Shakespeare, moving away from opening up the whole world of the play to children of all abilities.

PRACTICAL STRATEGIES

The joy of discovering Shakespeare's plays with young children is a collaborative unfolding of the heart of the play through its story, language and characters. It is not just about any one of these elements, but a complex interweaving within an active storytelling framework. Examples of the key elements of active storytelling follow here, giving an insight into how active storytelling works in practice. These examples of how to 'play out the play' are from a selection of Shakespeare's plays: *A Midsummer Night's Dream*, *Hamlet*, *Henry V*, *Macbeth*, *The Tempest* and *Twelfth Night*. The strategies have been extensively tried and tested with primary schoolchildren in many parts of Britain. They focus around the core activities of imaginative scene-setting; language games; role-play and improvisation. A full account of how to link these activities together – for the complete exploration of a whole play – can be found in the

Young Shakespeare Series – *Active Approaches to Shakespeare's Plays for the Under 12s* (Gordon and Geelan, various titles, 1994–8).

Central to a child's imaginative involvement in the drama is a strong visual sense of the characters and locations of the story. The entry into the drama begins in a similar way, whatever the play, with the teacher saying something along the lines of: 'Imagine we are going back in time hundreds of years to Scotland' (or 'Verona' or 'Athens'). This is historically non-specific, but encourages children to think about a world that is different from their own. In imaginative scene-setting activities the images are developed collectively by the group, each child contributing to the overall picture.

In *The Tempest* the children are asked to imagine they are on board a sailing ship hundreds of years ago. They are asked: 'What does it look like?' and 'What jobs might you, the sailors, be doing?' In groups the children then rehearse, as the sailors, a mimed scene of life on board the ship and perform this briefly to the other members of the class as their audience. Next, children are introduced to some of the characters who are on board the ship (using the sticky labels to identify individuals). These include King Alonso and other members of his royal party, some further characters from Shakespeare's play (Ferdinand, Sebastian, Antonio, Gonzalo, Stephano and Trinculo) and others created from the imaginations of the children (suggestions might include the Royal Cook, the Royal Doctor, the Royal Crown Holder).

From the start the children become involved in the world of the play by creating it via their own ideas and by using and remembering the names of the people or places as their first experience of using Shakespeare's language. In *The Tempest* this initial scene setting activity moves on to the children (now divided and identified as the two groups of royals and sailors) experiencing the storm as it hits their ship. Having discussed the sort of sounds that might be heard, the children themselves create a sound collage of the storm which moves, with a clear signal, into the introduction of the words of the sailors and royals. Short sections of language give the children a deeper experience of the storm scene as created by Shakespeare.

Sailors: All lost!
Royals: To prayers
Sailors: To prayers
Royals: All lost!
All: We split, we split, we split!
(*The Tempest*, Act I Scene i, Cambridge School Shakespeare, 1995)

The rhythm and length of these short sections of language are readily accessible to all of the children, through repetition.

In the banquet scene in *Macbeth*, children use longer sections of Shakespeare's language to deepen their understanding of the relationship between the central characters. Hooked thus far into the thriller-like unravelling of the plot through storytelling, collaborative improvisation, prediction and Shakespearean language, the children take a step further into the play. They guess that Macbeth will not return to the banqueting table because he can see Banquo's ghost sitting on his throne. The children, divided into two lines sitting opposite each other, enact the conversation between Macbeth and Lady Macbeth.

Macbeth 1:	Never shake thy gory locks at me.
Lady Macbeth 1:	Are you a man?
Macbeth 2:	Prithee see there!
Lady Macbeth 2:	This is the very painting of your fear.
Macbeth 3:	Behold. Look. Lo! How say you?
Lady Macbeth 3:	Why do you make such faces?
Macbeth 4:	If thou canst nod, speak too.
Lady Macbeth 4:	When all's done you look but on a stool.
Macbeth 5:	Avaunt and quit my sight.
Lady Macbeth 5:	Fie for shame.

(*Macbeth*, Act III Scene iv, Cambridge School Shakespeare, 1993)

Each group reads their words aloud in the correct sequence. The children participate in a discussion about the mood of the characters and how this is reflected in their
voice and facial expressions. The children then 'perform' the words in different ways:
sitting down, standing as they speak, in angry voices, hushed voices, Macbeth shocked
while Lady Macbeth is embarrassed and so on. Through speaking the language of
the characters, the children gain a real insight into the crisis at the banquet, as well
as the shifting relationship between the two protagonists. The following piece of
creative work – reproduced here with its original spellings and punctuation – was
written by two Year Six pupils in an outer London primary school as follow up to their
experience at the banquet and illustrates their personal engagement with the world of
the story.

'The Banquet'

And what a feast the cooks prepared,
For the Banquet fine,
Lords and Ladies from over the land,
Would come to the castle to dine.

Now the orchestras striking up,
Slowly ... slowly ... slowly.
Violins, cellos, flutes and drums
Playing music gaily.

Macbeth he was awaiting now,
For his guests to arrive at the castle.
The Duke and Duchess of Aire were first,
With their son Master Larsel.

And now the guests had all arrived,
The Banquet could now start.
Roast suckling lay before their eyes,
The smell hit their noses like a dart.

Meanwhile in great Burnam Wood,
Banquow rode down the path.
Two murderers sprang from behind the trees,
And stabbed him twice in the heart.

Back at the castle two men came in,
And ordered to see Macbeth,
'We have killed him!' They told him,
'We stabbed his heart, are you now pleased with his death!'

Macbeth after seeing the to grave men,
Turned back to the Banquet and then,
Screamed out loud and his face went all white,
As he saw the ghost of his friend.

'Don't shake your gory locks at me'
He said with a trembling voice.
'Just leave me alone I'm an innocent man,
I can't sit at the Banquet I have no choice.'

Lady Macbeth sent the guests all away.
With Macbeth she then had a word,
'You don't know how much you embarrassed me then,
When you screamed it just looked so absurd'.

'I saw a ghost' he said to her,
She said 'Your going insane,
There is nothing there I promise you
Your chair is just the same.'

'I know I saw him. I know I did'
He said to her that night.
'He was bleading and blood was all over his face,
And a knife was stuck in his heart.'

Lady Macbeth took his nonsense no more
She declared 'I'm going to bed.'
Macbeth thought he would do the same,
As he suffered an ache in the head.

This written work is inspired by the participation of the two authors in the banquet scene. Within a sophisticated (though not always perfectly metrical) rhyming structure, they have developed collaboratively a real sense of involvement with the scene – the setting, characters, emotions and language.

In *Henry V*, the children use Shakespearean language as they take on the persona of Henry addressing his troops outside Harfleur. Here Henry's speech has been pared down to give even the youngest child an insight into his mind.

1. Once more unto the breach, dear friends, once more
2. Or close the wall up with our English dead!
3. The blast of war blows in our ears
4. Imitate the action of the tiger
5. Stiffen the sinews
6. Conjure up the blood
7. Disguise fair nature with hard-favoured rage

8. On, on, you noblest English
9. Follow your spirit, and upon this charge cry
10. God for Harry, England and St. George!

(*King Henry V*, Act III Scene i, Cambridge School Shakespeare, 1993)

The words are distributed to nine groups. Line 10 of the speech – 'God for Harry, England and St George' – is a whole-group response. In this activity it often works well not only to explore different voices and emotions but also to encourage the groups to explore the physicality of the language. They can be encouraged to invent strong and warlike actions to accompany their words.

The natural progression from working on Shakespeare's language in groups is to divide a speech into enough sections for each individual child to have their own small piece of text. The choice of speech for this activity may be determined by a number of factors. The speech may serve as a stepping-stone into the mind or the imagination of a particular character. Alternatively it may offer insight into a predicament or situation. Some speeches are ideal for this activity because of the fullness of their descriptive powers, linguistic resources or powerful rhythm. Some speeches throw up possibilities of future hooks for the yet to be discovered strands of the developing story. The following speeches, when edited to approximately thirty short sections, work extremely well in the context of active storytelling : 'Yet here's a spot' (*Macbeth* V.i. lines 27–58); the Ghost speech (*Hamlet*, I.v. lines 9–90); 'Creeping murmur' (*King Henry V*, IV Chorus, lines 1–14); 'Ye elves' (*The Tempest*, V.i. lines 33–57); 'Now the hungry lion roars' (*A Midsummer Night's Dream*, V.i. lines 349–68); and 'I left no ring' (*Twelfth Night*, II.ii. lines 14–38).

TWELFTH NIGHT

In *Twelfth Night*, children who have no previous knowledge of the story imagine Viola's feelings and predict her future through exploring the 'I left no ring with her' speech. At this point in the developing drama the children have already met Viola and Sebastian (two labelled children), experienced the storm and the separation of the twins, met the members of Orsino and Olivia's households and helped Viola to make her decision about changing her identity to a man and becoming 'Cesario'.

In this language activity the teacher focuses on the moment in the play when Malvolio delivers Olivia's ring to 'Cesario' (really Viola). The teacher distributes the words of Viola's speech, divided up and written out on strips of paper, to each individual in the class. The extracts from the speech are short, to enable all of the children to feel confident about 'their' words. For some children the meaning of 'their' words is instantly clear. For others, they need to hear the words read aloud to them in sequence and in context before the meaning becomes clear. If children are encouraged to think of each extract as one piece of a jigsaw puzzle they will gain a sense of the whole when it is put together. The children delight in hearing their section read out and work out very quickly what has happened in the story. They discover the storyline directly through exploring Viola's words.

Children have fun with the words by speaking them and experimenting with different tone, volume, pace and emotion. The more children repeat 'their' words the more possessive they become about them. This is a collaborative language activity, not an academic exercise. It does not matter if children do not understand every word.

The insight into Viola's thoughts gained through this language activity enables children to move swiftly and naturally into role-playing where the child labelled as Viola takes suggestions from others about what she should do next. The children in the circle are encouraged to think carefully about Viola's options. Advice to Viola includes such suggestions as 'Tell the truth'; 'Tell Lady Olivia who you really are but ask her not to tell the Duke'; 'Run away'; 'Pretend that Cesario has had an accident and come back as Viola'; 'Go and find your brother Sebastian so that the lady can fall in love with him.' Time and time again in Shakespeare's plays children who have no knowledge of the plot predict what actually happens next through their own imaginative intuition.

This imaginative engagement is taken on into the development of improvised scenes involving all of the children. Some of these scenes reflect what Shakespeare himself wrote and others reflect the spirit of what we might call 'unwritten scenes'. In *Macbeth* they might be servants or guards waiting ceremoniously to greet King Duncan at Macbeth's castle; in *A Midsummer Night's Dream* groups of mechanicals making wedding presents for Theseus and Hippolyta; or, as below in *Hamlet*, entertainers and servants in King Claudius' court of Elsinore, preparing a grand evening of entertainments.

In the following 'unwritten' scene from *Hamlet* all of the children are organized into five small groups as cooks, guards, decorators, entertainers and actors, to prepare a formal presentation for the King and Queen. All of the groups, apart from the actors, are given free rein to devise and perform a short presentation. The actors work with Prince Hamlet and the adult facilitator on 'The Mousetrap'. Three of the actors are cast as the King, the Queen and the wicked nephew. These three will mime the story whilst the others in the group provide narration and sound effects. The children are given the framework for their story with the four following mimed scenes: (1) The Queen leaves the King to sleep in his orchard; (2) The wicked nephew pours poison in the sleeping King's ear; (3) The Queen discovers the body; (4) The Queen marries the wicked nephew. The children devise their own brief narration. While the five groups are busy rehearsing, Claudius is taken to one side and primed to shout 'stop' and storm out of the room when tapped on the shoulder, towards the end of 'The Mousetrap' play.

The evening of entertainments is formally announced. Everyone processes in and sits on the floor in front of Claudius's and Gertrude's thrones, facing a stage area. One by one the groups show their presentations on the stage. The actors are last. During the final scene, on cue, Claudius storms out. Everyone freezes and discusses the reactions and feelings of Claudius, Gertrude, Hamlet and the courtiers to these dramatic events.

Here, in *Hamlet*, a hook is created. Children are caught up in the tension and filled with a sense of purpose and excitement. They wait for the next twist in the tale, the next moral dilemma, the next relationship crisis or problem to solve. The more they are imaginatively inspired, the more they become committed to the world of the play.

It is the immediacy created by active storytelling that is so striking and so compelling for the children and the teacher. At the end of the play children are often unsure as to whether it was a true story because 'it felt real'. Such is the power of Shakespeare's stories even for the sophisticated children of our modern high-tech world. The quality of this imaginative involvement is enhanced by the special feeling of believing this world is being created uniquely by the children themselves. The words of a ten-year-old boy stay with me: 'At break time I have a big bunch of Shakespeare in my head. It keeps on going round in my mind.'

REFERENCES

DES (1988) *Report of the Committee of Inquiry into the Teaching of English Language*. London: HMSO (the Kingman Report).

DES (1989) *English for Ages 5 to 11: Proposals of the Secretary of State for Education and Science and the Secretary for Wales*. London: DES/NCC (known as the Cox Report).

DfEE (1998) *National Literacy Strategy*. London: HMSO.

Gibson, R. (1987) 'Primary Shakespeare', *Shakespeare and Schools Magazine*, No. 4, pp. 2–3.

Gibson, R. (series editor) *A Midsummer Night's Dream* (1992); *King Henry V* (1993); *Macbeth* (1993); *Twelfth Night* (1993); *Hamlet* (1994); *The Tempest* (1995); *King Henry IV* Pt 1 (1998). Cambridge School Shakespeare series. Cambridge: Cambridge University Press.

Gordon, S. (1997) *Active Approaches to A Midsummer Night's Dream*. London: Buttonhole Press.

Gordon, S. and Geelan, C. (1994) *Active Approaches to The Tempest*; (1998) *Active Approaches to Hamlet*, *Active Approaches to Henry V*, *Active Approaches to Macbeth* and *Active Approaches to Twelfth Night*. London: Buttonhole Press.

Chapter 11

'A Light in the Darkness': George Macdonald's Stories for Children

Mary Jane Drummond

In a beautiful essay written in 1882, George Macdonald sets out, with passion, his conviction of 'the necessity we are under to imagine'. 'The Imagination: its functions and its culture', is, by turns, lyrical, analytical, prophetical, polemic and reverent. Macdonald's position is made clear: without the redeeming power of the imagination, human society would be prey to terrible evils, 'Selfishness, avarice, sensuality, cruelty would flourish tenfold ...'. The necessity to imagine is an equally important imperative for children. Those who would 'quell ... the youthful imagination, (who) would crush and confine it ... will never lead them beyond dull facts – dull because their relations to each other, and the one life that works in them all, must remain undiscovered.' These tremendous claims are made in the context of Macdonald's definition of education, in a passage of great strength with which the essay opens:

> the end (of education) is a noble unrest, an ever renewed awaking from the dead, a ceaseless questioning of the past for the interpretation of the future, an urging on of the motions of life.
>
> (Macdonald, 1882a)

From this grand beginning Macdonald develops his central theme, demonstrating in every line the force of his trust in the power of the imagination to educate both young and old.

In the collection of essays in which 'The Imagination' appears, Macdonald is writing for his peers, as a deeply committed Christian, trained in his youth as a Congregational minister, though long since independent of any particular church or pulpit. During the 1860s and 1870s his work as a novelist brought him much fame, and two of his greatest books for children were also published during this time, *At the Back of the North Wind* (1871) and *The Princess and the Goblin* (1872). It is striking how clearly we hear, in these works, and, indeed, in all his writing for children, the voice of the child he once was. His life as an adult did not obliterate the traces and memories of childhood. So, for example, he writes of himself:

All sorts of bridges have been from very infancy a delight to me. For I am one of those who never got rid of their infantile predilections and to have once enjoyed making a mud bridge was to enjoy all bridges for ever.

(Macdonald, 1867a)

The authenticity of this enthusiasm is unmistakable; the abiding importance of the child's play to the child is convincingly conveyed. And equally in the stories, children's play is shown as a serious and significant occupation. Diamond, the little boy who is the hero of *At the Back of the North Wind*, is shown as

busy making a cave by the side of his mother's fire, with a broken chair, a three-legged stool, and a blanket, and then sitting in it.

Arthur Hughes's moving illustration of this solitary, not lonely, play gives an additional impetus to Macdonald's implicit argument – that young children's play is part of a grander project, no less than understanding themselves and the rest of the world. In another woodcut, Hughes shows us Diamond (whose father is a coachman) as Macdonald describes him:

driving two chairs harnessed to the baby's cradle; and if they did not go very fast, they went as fast as could be expected of the best chairs in the world, although one of them had only three legs and the other only half a back.

This passage assumes its full significance later in the story, when, during his father's illness, Diamond takes out the huge four-wheeled cab and plies for fares in the crush of the London streets. The play-driving by the fire, and the real-life driving for hire in the grey morning, are both part of the same purpose – the exploration and mastery of the world and what is in it, including Diamond himself.

In *Ranald Bannerman's Boyhood*, an adult novel which is in effect largely an autobiographical account of his own childhood, Macdonald's ability to see with a child's eyes, to speak with a child's words, is especially marked. At about the age of six, Ranald is sent to the little village school, kept by a dreadful old dame with a horrible dog; at the first opportunity Ranald runs away, but fearing to go home, hides in the hay in the barn till nightfall, and then finds himself most awfully abandoned:

in the vast hall of the silent night – alone: there lay the awfulness of it. I had never before known what the night was. The real sting of its fear lay in this – that there was nobody else in it. Everybody besides me was asleep all over the world, and had abandoned me to my fate, whatever might come out of the darkness to seize me.

(Macdonald, 1871b)

Fleeing from this terrible fear, Ranald runs home and falls asleep in his father's bed – the whole household is out searching for him. The blessed relief of waking in his father's arms is almost unbearably poignant, and utterly convincing. Macdonald can portray a child's sorrow and fear, his trials and misdeeds, quite as vividly as the joys and triumphs of his child heroes and heroines.

Macdonald's son, Greville, gives some fascinating insights into his own childhood, and his father's unusual theories of childrearing; Greville records that he had no schooling until he was eleven years old, and could then barely read. Macdonald gave him occasional lessons in Latin and Euclid, but, Greville comments dryly, 'they were not successful'. He continues, with a generosity of understanding just like his father's,

> My father's knowledge of his children's higher needs was surer than his ideas as to how the soil for them should be prepared: he knew the awakening of their imaginative sense was, after all, more important than academic grammar.
>
> (Macdonald, 1924)

What were these higher needs? How was the power of the imagination to be set to work in children? Macdonald explains in an extended and energetic metaphor:

> ... if we speak of direct means for the culture of the imagination, the whole is comprised in two words – food and exercise. If you want strong arms, take animal food, and row. Feed your imagination with food convenient for it, and exercise it, not in the contortions of the acrobat but in the movements of the gymnast.
>
> (Macdonald, 1882a)

Macdonald goes on to prescribe the necessary 'food'. First and foremost come books:

> the best must be set before the learner, that he may eat and not be satisfied; for the finest products of the imagination are the best nourishment for the beginnings of that imagination.

Here we see, in the most simple terms, the motivating force of Macdonald's work for children. His own imagination and all its creations – goblins, witches, fairies, grotesque monsters, angels, magical journeys and wonderful visions – were at the service of the children for whom he wrote; his purpose was essentially educative, but it is children's moral powers that are to be stimulated and strengthened, not their literary ones. The colossal concepts that Macdonald introduces in his fairy tales (love, pain, death, repentance, justice) are food for the spirit, not for the lesser faculties of science and rationality.

Here is Diamond talking to his mother about a song he has been singing to the baby.

> '*You* never made that song, Diamond', said his mother.
> 'No, mother ... But it's mine for all that.'
> 'What makes it yours?'
> 'I love it so.'
> 'Does loving a thing make it yours?'
> 'I think so, mother – at least more than anything else can. If I didn't love baby, she wouldn't be mine a bit. But I do love baby, and baby is my very own.'
> 'The baby's mine, Diamond.'
> 'That makes her the more mine, Mother.'
> 'How do you make that out?'
> 'Because you're mine, Mother.'

'Is that because you love me?'

'Yes, just because. Love makes the only myness', said Diamond.

Those who choose to dismiss passages like this as sentimental, sickly, evangelical (critics such as Humphrey Carpenter (1985), for example, who uses just such epithets) are missing the point. The words that Diamond speaks are not sweetmeats to be sucked and swallowed for sensual satisfaction; through this imaginary child's voice, Macdonald is offering his readers a hard and difficult truth, one that needs thinking about. The world and its people are not to be grasped with greedy hands or an acquisitive intelligence: 'the heart must open the door to the understanding' (Macdonald, 1882a).

In a dismissive paragraph, Carpenter (1985) characterizes Diamond as a poor, illiterate, half-invalid boy, suggesting he would be completely at home in the pages of contemporary Sunday School tracts: 'Macdonald the Congregationalist preacher has taken over from Macdonald the myth maker'. In my view, *At the Back of the North Wind* is neither tract nor myth but an urgent invitation to its readers to study the great moral lessons of humankind. Love is the subject of one of these lessons, and evil is another. A third, a key theme in all Macdonald's fantasies and fairy tales (and, indeed, in his adult novels too), is the necessity of spiritual growth. Diamond is seen as angelic and unearthly by the rowdy cabmen, who call him God's baby, to Diamond's private satisfaction, but for all his understanding, he has much to learn from the beautiful and terrible North Wind, in whose arms he flies through the skies at night. Curdie too, the miner's son who routs the goblins in *The Princess and the Goblin*, embarks on a journey of self-discovery, learning to listen to the words of the princess's mysterious great-great-grandmother (part fairy, part divinity), who teaches him the solemn lesson of growth into goodness.

Even at his most didactic however, Macdonald's serious purposes do not exclude the possibility of joy. Indeed, a phrase in the adult novel *Malcolm* (1875), 'the vital connection between joy and effort', suggests precisely how Macdonald sees the rewards of his characters' efforts, their trials and tribulations. The necessity of effort is to be understood in different ways. In the visible world of the story, in the images and symbols of Macdonald's imagination, there are goblins to subdue, monsters to be slain, perils to be braved, tests of courage to be endured; but there is also internal work to do. The hero Malcolm himself tries to explain this to the uncomprehending heroine Florimel (who has a particularly long and painful journey to make): 'thinking's the hardest work I ken'. Macdonald is emphatic that the way his characters must take is never the easy way. Tangle, for example, in *The Golden Key*, is shown the way on her journey by the Old Man of the Earth, who, stooping

> over the floor of the cave, raised a huge stone from it and left it leaning. It disclosed a great hole that went plumb-down. 'That is the way', he said.
>
> 'But there are no stairs.'
>
> 'You must throw yourself in. There is no other way.'
>
> (Macdonald, 1867b)

Early in Diamond's acquaintance with North Wind, he is trying to explain to her the importance of not breaking the law. 'The law would have some trouble to catch me!' retorts North Wind.

'But if it's not right, you know', said Diamond, 'that's no matter. You shouldn't do it.'
'I am so tall I am above *that* law', said the voice (of the North Wind).

This is the beginning of Diamond's slow discovery that North Wind is more than the ravishingly beautiful woman who folds him in her hair as she flies with him over the rooftops, more than the avenging angel who frightens the wicked old nurse with the gin bottle in the nursery cupboard, more than the destructive force behind the storm at sea, in which a ship is lost and the wretched passengers drown. In one of their last talks together, North Wind explains to Diamond that

> I don't think I am just what you fancy me to be. People call me dreadful names, and think they know all about me. But they don't. Sometimes they call me Bad Fortune, sometimes Evil Chance, sometimes Ruin, and they have another name for me which they think the most dreadful of all.

Macdonald is here a master of restraint: North Wind refuses to speak her dreadful name (which is, of course, Death), though for Macdonald, believing as he did, it is her most glorious and proudest title.

Colin Manlove's (1993) critical commentary on this story is helpful in disentangling the relation between Diamond's life in the London streets, Diamond's dreams, and his supernatural excursions by night with North Wind, (though I am not impressed by his banal phrase 'God's sub-vicar' to refer to this tremendous being). Manlove notes the names of the characters and places in the story, some with strange and other-wordly significance – Mr. Raymond (ray of the world), Paradise Row, Dulcimer (Diamond's baby sister). Other names and places belong in the everyday world – Mr Evans, Hoxton, Chiswick, Mrs Crump: the juxtaposition of these 'suggests the interpenetration of the ordinary and the divine'. North Wind is, in some passages, just an ordinary wind, who blows off chimney tops and sweeps the bad air away from the streets at night, but she is also, unmistakably, 'pain, suffering and death', imbued with something of God's 'dreadful love and power' (Manlove, 1993). *At the Back of the North Wind* ends, predictably, with Diamond's long-signalled death, though there are no conventional, heart-jerking descriptions of his grieving family. In the second of the Curdie books, *The Princess and Curdie* (1883), Macdonald spurns any predictable or conventional closure. Curdie and the Princess are indeed united in marriage, the goblins are finally vanquished, but far from living happily ever after, in the final chapter Curdie and the Princess die, childless and unmourned. The people choose a new king, whose insatiable greed for the precious ore in the rocks beneath the city weakens its foundations until

> one day at noon, when life was at its highest, the whole city fell with a roaring crash. The cries of men and the shrieks of women went up with its dust, and then there was a great silence.

'This is the Last Judgement', comments Carpenter.

> But it is a very strange Last Judgement: no-one is saved. In fact the conclusion of *The Princess and Curdie* is reminiscent not of the book of revelation, but of the fall of Sodom and Gomorrah.

(Carpenter, 1985)

This is a theme not normally considered a suitable subject for children's literature! But Macdonald never shrank from setting before his audience of children the grandest of ideas, including those the catechism labels the Four Last Things (Hell, Heaven, Death and Judgement). As Louis MacNeice (1965) puts it, 'He sees that the problem of evil really *is* a problem,' and he uses the stories to initiate children into the 'very serious moral issues' they embody. Macdonald dared to do this, in my view, because of his perspective on education, and his belief in the educability of the children for whom he wrote.

In *Castle Warlock* (1882b), one of the most powerful of the Scottish novels, Macdonald reiterates his claims for the imagination:

In the history of the world, the imagination has been oftener right than the intellect, and the things in which it has been right are of much the greater importance; only wherever Pegasus has shown the way through a bog, the pack-horse which followed got the praise of the discovery.

Macdonald's defence of the imagination (the great flying horse in this particularly splendid metaphor) takes a variety of forms but never varies in its intensity. In the essay on imagination, written in the same year (1882a), for example, there are other metaphors:

The region belonging to the pure intellect is straitened: the imagination labours to extend its territories, to give it room. She sweeps across the borders, searching out new lands into which she may guide her plodding brother. The imagination is the light which redeems from the darkness for the eyes of the understanding.

Macdonald is at pains to make it clear that it is children, as well as adults, who experience the brilliance of this light in the darkness:

We dare to claim for the true, childlike, humble imagination . . . that it possesses an insight into the very nature of things.

This insight, however, is not to be confused with certainty, a state of mind for which Macdonald expresses barely concealed contempt, preferring 'the large spaces of uncertainty' where the imagination has room to grow.

It is not the things we see the most clearly that influence us the most powerfully. Vivid visions of something beyond, something which eye has not seen nor ear heard, have far more influence than any logical sequences whereby the same things may be demonstrated to the intellect.

Macdonald goes on to explore more fully the contrasts he seeks to establish between knowledge and a sense of what is not known, between science and poetry, between certainty and hope, between 'the sphere hollowed out of the dark by the glimmering light of our knowledge' and 'the infinite lands of uncertainty.' In *Malcolm*, these distinctions are themselves given imaginative form and life in the person of Mr Graham, the teacher, who is both Malcolm's stern guide and counsellor on his spiritual journey, and a regular classroom teacher in whose school Malcolm has been a pupil. Mr Graham's view of teaching is clearly Macdonald's own; 'the one business of a teacher', he claims, is to join the battle for good and evil which is ever raging in the human mind, and to do so by

> leading fresh forces of truth into the field – forces composed as little as may be of the hireling troops of the intellect, and as much as possible of the native energies of the heart, imagination and conscience.

The teacher's task is to awaken the force of the child's imagination, the child's to exercise and grow ('exercise *is* growth', comments Macdonald in *Castle Warlock*, as his boy hero, Cosmo, dreams of how he will retrieve his family's lost fortunes and rebuild the castle of his ancestors). The food that will nourish this growth, this exercise, this spiritual strengthening, is itself provided by the power of the imagination. The nourishing effects of fairy tales, such as those Macdonald himself wrote, are directly attributable to the opportunities they offer children to do important kinds of work, thinking, feeling and understanding. In *What's Mine's Mine* (1886), a late and relatively unsuccessful Scottish novel, Macdonald contemptuously describes two sisters who have had no such opportunities:

> The human was not much developed in them; they understood nothing of their own beings; they had never had any difficulty with themselves – how could they understand others? They did not understand any human feeling – not even the silliness they called *love* – they had a feeling, or a feeling had them, till another feeling came and took its place ... They never came so near anything as to think about it ... They knew nothing of labour, nothing of danger, nothing of hunger, nothing of cold, nothing of sickness, nothing of loneliness. The realities of life, in their lowest forms as in their highest, were far from them.

The 'realities of life' are the stuff of Macdonald's fairy tales; his heroes and heroines, his princesses and paupers, are his counterblast to the perversion of humanity he depicts in these two ill-educated young women. Macdonald's fairy tale characters learn to understand themselves and others; they learn about love, labour, danger and loneliness. Most importantly, they learn the lesson of morality: 'It is necessary that all should understand and imagine the good' (from the concluding paragraph of the great essay on 'Imagination').

The effect of this particular view of reality, even within the most fantastic of his fairy tales, is singled out for comment by G. K. Chesterton, an ardent admirer of Macdonald's work. *The Princess and the Goblin* is set in an utterly fairy-tale castle, at the heart of a walled city, with dark stairs, underground passages, goblin caves, and the great-great-grandmother's turret chamber, which is furnished with mystic white doves and a fire of burning roses. It is of this book that Chesterton writes:

> Of all the stories I have read, including even all the novels of the same novelist, it remains the most real, the most like life.
>
> (Chesterton, 1924)

Louis MacNeice, another of Macdonald's admirers, speculates that the only way to understand this extraordinary claim is to suppose that Chesterton means that the life he discovers in *The Princess and the Goblin* is 'human life as seen, or felt, or divined from the inside'. This construction is not a particularly revealing one, side-stepping as it does MacNeice's other insights into Macdonald's intensely spiritual attitude to the universe, and his extraordinary mastery of the symbolic means by which to express it. His son Greville comes closer to a just estimate of his father's achievement in a passage in which he describes Macdonald's affinity with Ruskin:

> In both men, it was imagination that informed them of the truth before they set about its analysis. Because of their vision which sees beyond the horizon of things, both were adventurers, set out for an unknown yet to their eyes obvious land.
>
> (Macdonald, 1924)

Another critic, Humphrey Carpenter, is by no means so discerning, and very much less appreciative of Macdonald's work. *The Princess and the Goblin*, for example, he interprets as being 'as powerful a piece of religious teaching as ever came the way of a Sunday School child.' This disparaging judgement is, in my view, a mistaken one, in that Carpenter gives no credit to Macdonald's unique capacity to use themes and symbols from the spiritual universe, without ever descending to the level of a Sunday School tract. His adult novels are indeed largely concerned with the human journey towards God, but it is no Sunday School deity, no shepherd with his lambs, that concerns Macdonald. Mr Graham, the intensely religious teacher in *Malcolm*, is an eloquent mouthpiece for Macdonald's vision. Sent for by the wicked old marquis who is dying in agony, after a life of great cruelty and profligacy, Mr Graham speaks to him of God's will as better than his own. The angry marquis objects:

'That's all moonshine!'
'It *is* light, my lord.'

Macdonald's vision of the light is radiant; it shines in the darkness and redeems our understanding. His understanding of goodness is equally visionary; W. H. Auden (1973) calls his 'most extraordinary and precious gift' this ability to write about goodness in a way in which there is nothing phoney. He quotes Simone Weil on the same theme 'real good is always new, marvellous, intoxicating'. The importance of Macdonald's work for children is that it opens the door to what is new, marvellous and intoxicating, to those infinite spaces in which children can read, and feel, and imagine; as symbolists, as moralists, as compassionate loving beings, as students of truth and beauty.

REFERENCES

Auden, W. H. (1973) 'George Macdonald', in *Forewords and Afterwords*. London: Faber.

Carpenter, H. (1985) 'George Macdonald and the tender grandmother', in *Secret Gardens: A Study of the Golden Age of Children's Literature*. London: George Allen and Unwin.

Chesterton, G. K. (1924) Introduction in Greville Macdonald, *George Macdonald and his Wife*. London: George Allen and Unwin.

Macdonald, G. (1867a) *Annals of a Quiet Neighbourhood*. London: Hurst and Blackett.

Macdonald, G. (1867b) 'The Golden Key', in *Dealings with the Fairies*. London: Strahan and Co.

Macdonald, G. (1871a) *At the Back of the North Wind*. London: Strahan and Co.

Macdonald, G. (1871b) *Ranald Bannerman's Boyhood*. London: Strahan and Co.

Macdonald, G. (1872) *The Princess and the Goblin*. London: Strahan and Co.

Macdonald, G. (1875) *Malcolm*. London: Henry S. King.

Macdonald, G. (1882a) 'The Imagination: its functions and its culture', in *Orts*. London: Sampson Low.

Macdonald, G. (1882b) *Castle Warlock*. London: Sampson Low.

Macdonald, G. (1883) *The Princess and the Curdie*. London: Chatto and Windus.

Macdonald, G. (1886) *What's Mine's Mine*. London: Kegan Paul.

Macdonald, Greville (1924) *George Macdonald and his Wife*. London: George Allen and Unwin.

MacNeice, L. (1965) 'The Victorians', in *Varieties of Parable*. Cambridge: Cambridge University Press.

Manlove, C. (1993) 'George Macdonald', in *Scottish Fantasy Literature: A Critical Survey*. Edinburgh: Canongate Academic.

Chapter 12

Monologues and Spiels: The 'I' of my Poems

Michael Rosen

The word 'I' always poses some interesting problems in literature. In novels and short stories we are usually given some time and space to figure out who is talking to whom. This happens with Jim Hawkins in *Treasure Island* and as it takes a whole book for him to reveal the adventures we also get a good few chances to weigh up whether he is a 'reliable narrator' or not.

In poetry it can be an enigmatic business. When I started out writing I do not think I realized this. One of the first poems I wrote begins:

> I share my bedroom with my brother
> and I don't like it.
> His bed's by the window
> under my map of England's railways
> that has a hole in just above Leicester
> where Tony Sanders, he says,
> killed a Roman centurion
> with the Radio Times.
>
> (Rosen, 1974)

I was twenty at the time and was no longer sharing my bedroom with him! So in one sense the statement is an untruth – the kind of untruth we call Literature. But, I can honestly say, yes I did once share a bedroom with my brother and the poem was an effort on my part to represent what it had felt like ten years or so earlier. In other words the text follows a convention that we have come to accept. A poem can begin with an 'I', it can be in the present tense and as readers we can believe that the writer is representing the thoughts of a previous 'I'. Obviously I was by no means the first poet to do this, nor even the first poet for children to do it. Robert Louis Stevenson's *A Child's Garden of Verses* seems to be playing the same game. Both for internal and external reasons, we have come to think of that book as largely autobiographical thereby making the 'I' statements in the poems the same peculiar falsehoods that I've often written as with: 'I'm the youngest in our house . . . ' (from *Wouldn't You Like to Know*, 1977); 'We sit down to eat/and the potato's a bit hot . . . ' (from *The Hypnotiser*, 1988) and so on.

I suppose we accept these ways of writing because, like many literary conventions, they are ways of inviting readers to play a game: 'just imagine if this were true . . . ' We only agree to play because the experience of playing has a track record of being enjoyable. Too many setbacks on the road of trying to learn the rules and we give up. I know this to my own cost because when my first book of poems appeared *Mind Your Own Business* (Rosen, 1974), there were plenty of people who were genuinely quite confused about what it was. Strange untitled snippets of 'chopped-up prose' seemed scattered through a book, with large chunks of white space, amidst wonderful but uncaptioned cartoons by Quentin Blake. At the time, I was arrogant and un-self-aware enough to imagine that such a production would pose few problems to the sophisticated readership of, say, *Voices* edited by Geoffrey Summerfield for Penguin Educational. Thus my blithe, uncontextualised 'I'.

Later I retreated. Where Stevenson had boldly trodden, creating his fragmentary verse autobiography in the voice of a child, addressed to children, I now took one step back. In *Quick Let's Get Out of Here* (Rosen, 1983) I decided to be more direct. Experiences that I had described in that present tense voice, were pushed back into a past. I began poems with phrases like 'When I was seven . . . ' 'Me, my dad/and my brother/we were looking through the old photos . . . ' and 'Nearly every morning/my brother would lie in bed . . . '

What's more, I put titles on the poems. The only present-tense poems in the book are the ones that were actually representations of very recent experiences, mostly about bringing up my son Eddie. This shift came about in very large part as a consequence of several years of close contact with my audience: children and teachers in schools, including finding ways of performing pieces that were more related to the spiels and monologues of stand-up comedy routines. So what has happened is that in the nine years or so between the two books, the 'persona' of the poems shifts. In the first the persona is about ten years old, and in the second he's about 35.

Now let's leap forward another ten years or so to *You Wait Till I'm Older Than You* (Rosen, 1996). The persona has shifted back. Once again, the 'I' is mostly the ten-year-old me. Oddly, the reason for the shift is the same even though it's in the opposite direction. I now have the fantastic luxury and honour of being a writer who can address an audience that is in some way or another already 'author-ready'. Anyone who writes scripts for *Coronation Street* or any famous comedian like Lenny Henry or Jasper Carrott is working to an audience that is already 'competent' in reading them. There are expectations and hopes in that audience's mind. In my case, it's teachers who are the author-ready ones and it's they who are often the first distributors of my work. So what happened when I was getting *You Wait Till I'm Older Than You* ready was that Rosemary Stones, then editor at Penguin Children's Books, pointed out that I could make the poems about my childhood consistent by speaking with that voice once again. In fact, *The Hypnotiser* several years earlier had done this too, but this time I made a conscious decision to reproduce that ten-year-old persona again. And I did it in the knowledge that now it wouldn't pose the problems that cropped up with that first book. Because of their collective competencies in reading me, I felt that it was quite likely that I wouldn't leave too many people scratching their heads.

But there are other 'I's in my poems:

Down behind the dustbin
I met a dog called Jim.
He didn't know me
and I didn't know him.

I can honestly put my hand on my heart and tell you that this poem is an utter untruth. I have never met a dog called Jim, either behind a dustbin or anywhere else. This whole ghastly business was unravelled when I performed the poem in front of a group of ten-year-olds and one of them called out: 'How did you know his name was Jim, then?' And I had no answer to that. In a flash it was obvious to the whole audience I had lied. And then I compounded the perjury by saying:

Down behind the dustbin
I met a dog called Nicola
She looked a bit like an onion
so I thought that I would pickle 'er.

Now who is this 'I'? In one sense it's me, because it comes with my signature. But in another sense it's really an intertextual 'I'. It's the 'I' of nonsense poetry, especially that of Spike Milligan. Adventures in the outside world are shown as happening to a quasi-real person, and for it to be nonsense, the adventures are absurd, full of transformations, surprises and impossible changes. Edward Lear and Lewis Carroll had explored the territory by using mythical and not-so-mythical creatures wandering about in strange landscapes. I think of many of them as mock-colonial excursions in the outer regions of a pseudo-British Empire. Milligan, who cut his teeth on similar mock-colonial discourse in the Goon Shows, helped create the persona of a questioning and confused 'I' wandering about in an absurd world. The 'I' of this space then has already been created for writers like me. We can be 'I's doing these absurd things too.

In *Michael Rosen's Book of Nonsense* (1997) this was the 'I' that I pursued. Looking back on how I wrote it, I can see that in a sense I borrowed the nonsense 'I' and asked it to exist in a world made up of beings and objects transformed out of my real world. This is not as complex as it sounds – anyone listening to children in free play and dialogue does it all the time. So I ended up writing:

My face fell off my head
and landed on the floor,
wriggled about awhile
then galloped out the door.

It scared a cat in the yard.
It ate some bread and jam.
It fell into a puddle –
now I don't know who I am.
                    (Rosen, 1997)

So it was, that having created this absurd 'I', I could do so much to it, in the end it wasn't even sure that it existed!

Elsewhere in my poems I've also been able to try out that ventriloquist's act so beloved of poets: the dramatic monologue. Once poets figured out that you could remove a character from a drama and give him or her or it a speech, new possibilities emerged. Whether this 'drama' existed as a play, or as a historical moment, or as something to be divined from the context of the monologue itself was entirely up to the poet. Browning put words into the mouth of a rather disgusting Duke and we slowly figure out from 'his own' words that he's done in the Duchess. But they also exist in children's playground rhymes:

> I like coffee
> I like tea
> I like Shirley
> in with me ...

or

> Over the garden wall
> I let my baby fall
> my mother came out
> she gave me a clout
> she gave me another
> to match the other
> over the garden wall ...

So at various times in my poems 'I' have been a wasp stuck in a wasp trap, a lamp-post, a guide to a tower block, a runaway hamburger and more recently, Yum-yum who eats games of tennis.

Mostly I've avoided the 'I' of a child I've never been. I'm not sure why. It's not any point of principle. I think perhaps it was about wanting to get my old juvenile 'I' off my chest first before experimenting with anyone else's. More recently I have tried it a little more, imagining myself to be like one of my own children responding to things as with 'Great Day' in *You Wait* which begins:

> Can't find the bathroom
> Can't find my socks
> Can't find the corn-flakes
> Can't find the lunch-box ...
>   (Rosen, 1996)

and from the same collection:

> Sweetshop
>
> do you think there's a sweetshop here?
> are we going to the sweetshop?
> when are we going to the sweetshop?
> will you take me to the sweetshop?

and so on.

Perhaps more of these will appear, though there's part of me that's slightly worried that they might undermine what has been something of an autobiographical project. I like that old authentic 'I' trying to pin down the feeling and irony of everyday life as I've lived it and these other 'I's seem less attached to reality. But then, another side of me likes the idea of using language for free play, pushing it around to see what crops up. If the starting point is a nonsense 'I', or another persona's 'I' then that can take me into parts of my consciousness that I didn't even know existed.

REFERENCES

Rosen, M. (1974) *Mind Your Own Business*. London: Andre Deutsch Ltd.

Rosen, M. (1977) *Wouldn't You Like to Know*. London: Andre Deutsch Ltd.

Rosen, M. (1983) *Quick Let's Get Out Of Here*. London: Andre Deutsch Ltd.

Rosen, M. (1988) *The Hypnotiser*. London: Andre Deutsch Ltd.

Rosen, M. (1996) *You Wait Till I'm Older Than You*. London: Viking.

Rosen, M. (1997) *Michael Rosen's Book of Nonsense*. Hove: Macdonald Young Books.

V

New Narratives

Chapter 13

Past Perfect and Future Conditional: The Challenge of New Texts

Eve Bearne

> Perfection will never be reached; but to recognise a period of transformation when it comes, and to adapt themselves honestly and rationally to its laws, is perhaps the nearest approach to perfection of which men and nations are capable. No habits or attachments should prevent their trying to do this; nor in the long run can they.
>
> (Arnold, 1861)

At the turn of the century there is an urge to survey all that has happened and recognize the patterns of change and continuity during the last hundred years or so. However, the rosy glow of nostalgia is often a snare and a delusion – the 'habits and attachments' that Arnold warns of can significantly hold us back. Whilst there is satisfaction from seeing that some things do not change, but gain grace and dignity with age, looking backwards can be a dangerous thing to do when entering a changing landscape. At the start of the twenty-first century we are experiencing major shifts in the production and reception of literacy, every bit as significant for the population as the changes brought about by the industrial revolution which fed Matthew Arnold's thoughts. His words are a reminder that whilst striving for perfection is an acceptable, if not praiseworthy notion, more often than not we have to be adaptable, to shift our thinking to accommodate those things which happen around us. This is particularly relevant when considering reading, which is continually under scrutiny and embraces both change and continuity.

The narratives we meet now come in a sometimes bewildering array of forms. As the century turns, new technology has increased the number and type of pictorial and cinematic texts as well as bred entirely new forms of text on computers. Children are not starved of traditional types of text; there are still the sequential stories which helped many of us become assured and hungry readers. There are still the poems which tell of everyday and other-worldly events; there are still the comics, fast becoming recognized as important in shaping readers and their preferences and there are still films, particularly cartoon films, which many of us enjoyed when young. There are picture storybooks and there is television, the source of many familiar narratives. Then there are newer forms of story which many of us did not meet when young: graphic novels, CD-ROMs, computer games and virtual reality representations as well as a massive proliferation of other visual texts. There are also innovative formats for the novel, such as *Spring-Heeled Jack* by Philip Pullman (1989) which is fragmented, with multimodal pages, and quirky organization, which add to the vast range of texts available to young readers.

A list like this shows just how rich the treasure store of narrative is, yet in the eyes of many adults the range seems threatening and just too much to contemplate. There is evidence of adults withdrawing from the mediation of reading new types of texts with children, over-faced by the demands of getting to grips with them. Young readers confidently tackle demanding visual texts leaving adults to wonder what there is in it for them when sharing the reading. It is impossible to read a wordless picture book, a graphic novel or a CD-ROM *to* a child; such texts demand a shift towards reading *with* as well as *to* children.

However, it is only partly because of the relative newness and unfamiliarity of the forms that adults resist accepting them as valuable parts of the reading diet. There is often an unthinking negative reaction to the idea of young people being encouraged to read comics, magazines and formula-narratives, and now computer and video games, because they fall into the loose category of 'popular culture'. It is reminiscent of the old aphorism about a puritan being a person who believes that somehow, somewhere, someone might be having fun. The link between these forms of text and pleasure, play and enjoyment is feared as anti-educational. And yet in the middle of the 18th-century, John Newbery referred to children's books as offering 'instruction through delight' (Newbery in Harvey Darton, 1932) and John Rowe Townsend reminds us that John Locke 'argued that children should be taught by kindness rather than the rod and should "play themselves into that which others are whipp'd for" ' (Townsend, 1996). In this aspect of children's reading experience, particularly, it seems that there is a significant gap between newly emerging views of the importance of playful texts to the development of literacy and the traditional anxieties associated with how best to help children become readers. Target-setting and pacy teaching style seem to run counter to delight, and conversations between parents and teachers rarely involve discussions of the value and pleasure derived from reading popular texts; more often the adults express concern that this is not 'real reading'. Yet as Geoff Fenwick (1998) points out in *The Beano-Dandy Phenomenon*, 'Many adults have claimed that an enjoyment of comics set them on the road to effective reading'. More dialogue about shared enjoyment (and the educational value) of *The Beano* or *The Simpsons* might be one very powerful way of bridging the gap between different views about reading.

LEAVING YOUNG READERS TO IT

Worries about popular texts are most acute when teachers discuss the new narratives of children's computer and video games, making it difficult to separate attitudes to popular culture in the classroom from attitudes to computer-based texts. It is equally difficult to disentangle the historically derived sense (in the UK at least) that written words are more valuable and harder to understand than pictures, from the acknowledgement of the pleasures derived and observed when adults and children, or sometimes adults on their own, view picture books, videos and soap opera. It seems paradoxical: adults holding opposing views in parallel – that there is enjoyment to be gained from popular forms of narrative but that such texts are in some way less valuable in contributing to the process of becoming a discriminating reader.

In a research project carried out by Jack Sanger and his team into interactive screen-based technologies used in the home and school (computer games, personal computers, video games and videos themselves) it became clear that on the whole teachers felt ill at ease with the new popular texts of video and computer technology. Young readers are being expected to grow up 'without any critical debate from parents or teachers concerning the production, presentation or content of many of the programs and videos with which they interact'. The research found that 'The initial response of most teachers to questions from our team about these media, and about popular culture as a whole, was one of disapproval' (Sanger *et al.*, 1997). These findings point to the complexity of any enquiry into the relationship between adults, children and interactive technology texts. Despite the fact that many of the new computer texts are described as 'edutainment', linking entertainment and education in a similar way to Newbery and Locke (Richards, 1998), there is strong resistance to anything which seems to challenge 'habits and attachments' to the texts which teachers see as valuable.

Of course, children's induction and education into literacy is not just the school's or teachers' domain and responsibility; homes play a critically important part. Sanger's researchers interviewed parents over a period of time. They found that, at first, parents also indicated disapproval of entertainment technology but that:

> Whilst teachers maintained their disapproval throughout their interviews, some parents shifted position considerably within their interviews once they realised that the inter-viewers were neutral on the issue ... their original assumptions being that the research was setting out to prove that *the technology concerned was harmful*. But during inter-views, they often reversed this position.
>
> (Sanger *et al.*, 1997)

The difference in attitudes, Sanger concludes, is related to questions like 'What should childhood involve? What is good for children and what is bad?' These are absolutely sound questions which have permeated adults' views on texts for children for centuries. They are questions which ought to be asked in any responsible nation (Bearne, 1996). However, they need also to be articulated and answered in a way which helps all adults mediate and discuss new types of texts with children. Perhaps the most chilling finding of Sanger's research was not that there was residual, and sometimes unthinking, resistance to popular new forms of narrative, but that despite adults' attitudes, 'There was an overall feeling that children are being left to drift in a leisure world of growing technological sophistication' (Sanger *et al.*, 1997).

The research indicated what can be observed in many classrooms – handing over the use of new technology to the children because they are often more adept than the adults. This is understandable and, indeed, has elements of genuine recognition of children's strengths and knowledge. However, it also signals adults' attitudes very clearly. It is true of parents as well as teachers, but since teachers educate the parents of the next generation, their role is central in demonstrating the inclusion of new types of text in a definition of what becoming a discriminating reader might mean.

Imagine this: a teacher walks into a classroom holding a book and says to the class, 'I don't know how to open this; you'll have to do it, you're better at it than I am anyway'. From that point on the teacher simply watches the children opening the book and reading the text, taking little further part in the process.

Would that ever happen?

LEARNING THE LANGUAGE

> The human crisis is always a crisis of understanding: what we genuinely understand, we can do.
>
> (Williams, 1958)

If we do not come to understand the new types of text which our children are faced with every day, then we are likely to reach crisis. Even if we cannot get to grips with the machinery ourselves, we must begin to have conversations about the texts children read and view. Williams indicates the importance of reflective talk:

> ... our vocabulary, the language we use to inquire into and negotiate our actions, is no secondary factor, but a practical and radical element in itself. To take a meaning from experience, and to try to make it active, is in fact our process of growth. Some of these meanings we receive and recreate. Others we must make ourselves and try to communicate.

In terms of the latest thinking about reading, this makes very good sense. Once readers develop a metalanguage through which to talk about texts they are in a position to say – and think – even more. However, as Williams points out, 'Active reception, and living response, depend in their turn on an effective community of experience'. Such a community can only be forged by shared experience. It seems vital that we try to tackle new kinds of reading, reversing Williams' assertion and reminding ourselves that 'what we can do, we understand' – and can talk about in an informed way. This means that not only do we need to learn how to read the range of texts which children will meet but also how to talk about them. Since many of the new forms of text are more frequently read in the home, this means finding out just what children choose to read, as well as what they learn from their chosen texts, including multimedia texts. Sometimes, however, finding out about home reading experience can be quite a shock. In answering a questionnaire about home and school reading, one Year 5/6 class in a Cambridge primary school (16 boys and 17 girls) recorded some interesting responses to questions about reading at home.[1] The boys indicated reading a much wider range of texts at home than the girls did. At the same time, the responses showed both boys and girls reading twice as many genres of text at home than they did in school. One other significant aspect of the survey was the extent (and types) of television, video and computer reading which these young people reported. Whilst boys and girls recorded equal incidences of watching children's TV (the largest category) and adult programmes, mostly sit-coms, twice as many girls watched soaps as boys and very few girls noted watching sport on television, whereas this was the second largest category for boys.

In a much fuller survey carried out in a secondary school in Essex, Nigel Spratt and Ruth Sturdy found that in response to the question *Do you like reading?*, more girls than boys in Years 7, 8 and 9 said that they liked reading; however, Year 10 girls recorded a much higher 'no' response than the boys (Spratt and Sturdy, 1998). It seemed that the reading demands of different subjects for GCSE – mostly from textbooks – were the reason for this significant shift in their attitudes towards reading. This prompted the teachers to extend their survey to a much fuller investigation of genre and reading tastes, both at school and at home. The genre preferences of Years 7 to 10 indicate a marked increase in comic and magazine reading and a decline in non-fiction reading, particularly among the girls as they grow older.

These responses led to some focused attention on particular groups of readers, tracking pupils in order to record the kinds of reading demands made on them across the curriculum as they moved through their weekly lessons. Interviews with the pupils revealed that they felt that the teachers had stopped helping them with their reading by the time they reached Year 9. This perception had particular significance for those pupils who were finding difficulties with the different reading demands of the curriculum. None of this comes as a surprise, but it certainly raises some sharp issues about what teachers need to do. One 'practical and radical' move would be to get to grips with the language of new forms of text; to teach pupils how to describe, analyse and evaluate new forms of text, not just in lessons called 'media studies' but as part of a wider approach to reading. Otherwise, it will be no surprise to find that young readers feel that their teachers have stopped helping them with reading, leaving them adrift with no experience of discussing the structures, content and relative merits of popular, and other, forms of text.

In their introduction to *The Grammar of Visual Design* (1996), Gunther Kress and Theo van Leeuwen explain that they hesitated over the title because 'grammar' often suggests the idea of rules. They draw on the work of the linguist Michael Halliday to take the idea further:

> Grammar goes beyond the formal rules of correctness. It is a means of representing patterns of experience ... It enables human beings to build a mental picture of reality, to make sense of their experience of what goes on around them and inside them.
>
> (Halliday, 1985)

Here, Halliday captures an important element of being a reader – the interplay between the inner life of the imagination and an appreciation of the texts which are on offer – as well as the contexts in which they are presented. Adults often assert that a visual representation of a text prevents the full play of the imagination. This is not always so. After thought and some experience of the complexity of visual texts it becomes clear that reading pictorial text is as challenging as reading verbal text; but it is different. Anthony Browne argues for a compulsory element of education which stresses the visual, since children generally have a more developed visual awareness than adults which is driven out of them by 'a terrible pressure ... to leave pictures behind and to grow into words'. He points out that illustrations and pictorial text 'don't just happen by chance':

> The placing of figures in space and in relation to others, the use of colour and light all help to express emotion and tell the story. It's this aspect of picture books that fascinates me: the gap that exists between the image and the words, the gap that has to be filled by the child's imagination.
>
> (Browne, 1997)

There is no doubt that taking meaning from the experience of reading visual texts and trying to make it active, as Raymond Williams suggests, is, indeed, a 'process of growth'. As he points out, being able to talk about the representations of visual experience is critical, even more critical at this period of transformation in visual communication. Kress and van Leeuwen imagine that there will come a time when being visually literate will carry social value in a similar way to verbal literacy today. This will mean teachers paying attention to – and teaching – the grammar of visual design. However, Kress and van Leeuwen do not see this as necessarily constraining, since, 'Teaching the rules of writing has not meant the end of creative uses of language in literature and elsewhere'. They point out that:

> Just as the grammar creatively employed by poets and novelists is, in the end, the same grammar we use when writing letters, memos, reports, so the 'grammar of visual design', creatively employed by artists is, in the end, the same grammar we need when producing layouts, images, diagrams.
>
> (Kress and van Leeuwen, 1996)

This means that in the same way that verbal language is constructed in smaller units like the sentence and the larger discourse units, so any analysis of the grammar of visual design will need to take account not only of the individual items within a particular image, but also of the larger structures of the visual text – the overall grammar of a picture book, video game, CD-ROM or magazine double-page spread, for example. Equally, just as verbal language reflects aspects of the culture in which it is used, so visual language is culture specific and needs to be looked at within its social and cultural contexts.

PATHWAYS THROUGH TEXTS

The grammars of larger texts give their structure; they also offer signposts to guide the reader through visual, verbal, multimedia or multimodal texts. Very often, perceptions of texts have a significant spatial element. The following extract from a novel by the Native American poet and novelist Sherman Alexie takes a new look at reading and text structure:

> John had known he wanted to go to college when he was three years old. He had learned to read then, and reading taught him everything he needed to know about life inside the reservation. He picked up a book before he could read, when the words were still a mess of ink and implications, and somehow understood the purpose of a paragraph. The paragraph was a fence that had words. All the words inside a paragraph had a reason for being together. They shared a common history. John began to see the whole world in paragraphs. He knew the United States was a paragraph within the world. He knew his reservation was a paragraph within the United States. His house was a paragraph distinct from the houses to the west and north. Inside the house his mother was a paragraph, completely separate from the paragraph of John. (Alexie, 1997)

The visual shape of the paragraph on the page became a symbol of separateness within a whole space for Alexie and his central character John. When my niece Kim was

Figure 13.1

four and could not yet read for herself, she used to choose books with dialogue, indicated by line arrangement and inverted commas, because she liked me to 'do all the voices'. Seven-year-old Peter explained that his invented 'snowman language' followed a pathway from left to right then from right to left on the following line (see Figure 13.1). He pointed out that it was 'like Arabic' and when I asked him how he knew about such a language, he explained that his mother had told him about it but he had also seen it on television. Some children notice and think not only about the spatial arrangements of text on the page but also about directionality and print as symbolic of language even before they can read. It is worth discussing all of these aspects of reading with children rather than staying with the expectations of continuous print. In particular, it is worth discussing – and teaching – the varied pathways taken as texts are read and understood.

The idea of a 'reading path' describes the way in which the organisation or design of a page of text encourages a particular direction of eye movement in reading it. This concept has been developed particularly in theories of multimodal texts (Kress and van Leeuwen, 1996). The text-maker quite deliberately sets out to guide the eye through a particular path associated with the meanings the text is designed to convey. This does not mean, of course, that the reader will necessarily take this pathway, but there seem to be some useful generalities. In a picture book, for example, the eye almost always goes to the right-hand page, then backtracks to the left and eventually back to the right so that the image on the right-hand page is read twice. If print were placed on the right and pictorial text on the left, this would indicate the relative salience ascribed to each mode of representation. In complex pictorial text like a graphic novel, the reading pathway might move from an image at centre or right to the periphery of the page; it might take the eye in a zigzag movement from top left to bottom right as in print text, or offer a full double-page image which can be read radially. There would be other possible routes, too.

Such pathways for reading are already part of the existing repertoire of experienced readers' ways in to visual texts, yet are rarely made explicit or taught as part of the reading process. The traditional emphasis on verbal text tends to distract from the importance of developing understanding of a range of pathways possible within the organization of pictorially designed layout.

In getting to grips with the constructedness of multimedia and multimodal texts, there are not only some existing experiences to draw on but also an awareness of concepts and knowledge involved in talking about media texts. 'Framing' within a cinematic or other media context is a familiar idea but is becoming more important to deal with explicitly as we pay attention to comics and comic-book formats for other texts, graphic novels and wordless picture books. The relationship between the frames is equally important as the juxtapositions create text cohesion and help to direct the narrative (Rowe, 1996). Within images, too, there are specific aspects which merit attention as they contribute to the meaning of the text as a whole. *Vectors*, leading the eye in an image, indicate salience – what is important; this might be a relationship between characters or drawing attention to an object which carries significance. They may be formed by angles in the image, by direction of lines of objects such as tree branches, arms, railway lines or the eye gaze between characters. Characters' eye gaze within an image can be described as *demands* and *offers* referring to the relationship between the direction of gaze and the reader/viewer. The vectors track the imagined lines of gaze; a demand image has the character looking directly at the reader or with vectors intersecting just behind/above/beside the reader's head, making a direct link with the audience, whereas an offer image would show the character looking inward to somewhere within the picture. Vectors do not simply contribute to the construction of meaning within an individual image, however; they are also part of the cohesive structure of visual narratives, driving the narrative forward or interrupting it, to signal the narrative pathway. In CD-ROM texts there is often a metafictive character or a series of icons to direct our gaze in certain ways and to suggest to the reader the possible pathways through the text.

The reader of a picture book or pictorially sophisticated graphic novel like the new *Batman* series (Robinson and Estes, 1996) has to make some choices about pathways through the text, and may have to work very hard to construct the narrative. However, in CD-ROM texts there is a *requirement* to make interventions. Rather than reading a linear narrative each reader constructs an individual and personal pathway through the hypertext where active connections are made between different parts of the text. Even a very young reader of the CD-ROM of Dr Seuss' *Green Eggs and Ham*, for example, does not have to follow a direct pathway determined by the narrator; there is some flexibility in direction as the reader makes choices in working with the hypertext, deciding which hot spot to click on and which part of the narrative to pursue. This does not necessarily signal a new way of reading. In making meaning of either book-based or computer-based visual texts, there is a similar dynamic relationship between the reader and the text. When someone is reading CD-ROM texts this becomes overt and observable.

Making meaning from disparate images is part of a developed narrative-making ability which draws on experience of the grammatical cohesion of texts. In describing cohesion in multimodal or multimedia texts, Kress and van Leeuwen use Halliday's description of the information structure of a clause where the opening part contains the known or 'given' and the later part is the 'new' information:

In language, as in visual communication, this is not a constituent structure, with strong framing between the elements, but a gradual, wave-like movement from left to right (or rather, from 'before' to 'after', since in language we are dealing with temporally integrated texts).

(Kress and van Leeuwen, 1996)

Similarly, in the spatially integrated design of Western visual texts, the 'given' is on the left and the 'new' on the right; this makes for the narrative drive of a picture book, for example. Each 'new' becomes the 'given' of the following page, giving the narrative impetus and adding to the cohesion of the text. A grammatical pattern like this can equally well inform analysis of film, comic-book format, graphic novels and CD-ROM texts. Movement from the left into the central area of the screen or page and towards the right, allied with other framing devices, contributes to the culturally developed conventions of text cohesion in visual narratives.

TRANSFORMING TEXTS

The transformation of a story from one set of media-specific codes to another involves a change of narrative structure.

(Parker, 1999)

The development of television, video and communications technology gives greater scope for presenting different versions of the same story. Books appear as films; television series generate books. However, a different version of a text – a 'recontextualisation' – can be distasteful to some readers who feel that their imagined experience of a story has been taken over by someone else's visual interpretation. Nonetheless, there are times when another presentation can illuminate the verbal text. The term 'recontextualisation' offers a different way of talking about 'versions' of known texts; it helps us to understand that for example, the film of *The Secret Garden* is a text in its own right, not just a (sometimes 'unsatisfactory') use of the book text. David Parker's research into primary school pupils adapting a text from print into a moving image medium strongly suggests that such transformations aid reading development. His work shows that creating different forms of the same story can give young readers/viewers 'greater "cognitive space" to construct meanings' as they decide on the elements which best fit either a written or film narrative. Their sharpened awareness of the ways in which words or images create atmosphere, tension or narrative suspense, for example, further enriches their own story writing (Parker, 1999).

Looking carefully at narrative structures helps those younger readers to take their writing further. In a series of literature lessons with older pupils, Richard Bain sees value in the dynamic possibilities of computer hypertext for their own reading and writing. He uses the opportunities offered to 'help pupils go beyond the superficial skimming that can result from Internet "surfing", and to use the structure of hypertext to take the reading deeper into an understanding of a text' (Bain, 1999). He takes on issues of text cohesion, encouraging pupils to construct hyperpoems and flexible stories by using existing poetry, in this case by Blake, which he put on to a website, thus allowing the readers to move in and out of the text, highlighting and selecting parts as they chose. As Kress points out:

> Reading is not simply the assimilation of meaning, the absorption or acquisition of meaning as the result of a straightforward act of decoding. Reading is a transformative action, in which the reader makes sense of the signs provided to her or him within a frame of reference of their own experience, and guided by their interest at the point of reading. (Kress, 1997)

Such 'recontextualisations' as Richard Bain encourages his students to make offer another dimension to the Bakhtinian idea of the *heteroglossia* of texts. Bakhtin introduced this term to describe how texts are made up of 'many voices' from the different genres, dialects and styles within a language. These all reverberate with previously acquired knowledge and experience – cultural, social, linguistic, literary, visual and connotative – adding texture and textual complexity (Bakhtin, 1981). For Bakhtin, this concept helped to describe the dynamic relationship between reader and text as meaning is constructed; it acts as a counter to the idea of a text having a single authoritative 'meaning'. Richard Bain's students added their own voices to the already existing heteroglossia of Blake's poetry, mixing their young voices with Blake's older cadences.

In another example, Darryl, in Year 3, adds his voice to the persuasive tones of advertising, showing just how powerful transformation can be when interest is engaged. His teacher had encouraged him to use his knowledge of comic-style texts and video games to continue writing in school the comics he wrote at home.[2] In these comics he demonstrated considerable knowledge of the organization of picture and texts and their distinctive uses of vocabulary as his video game review shows (see Figure 13.2). His reading of multimodal and multimedia text has richly fed him with knowledge both of the grammar of layout and choice of font associated with a designed text like an advertisement and the grammar of complex sentences: 'if you think this is dull … ' Darryl's assurance with the persuasive voice of advertising emphasizes the fact that children bring into the classroom knowledge of all kinds of new texts which can often be unacknowledged. At the same time as they are learning the 100 basic words, children are capable of quoting from, for example, the Genie's song in the Disney version of *Aladdin*: 'The ever-impressive, the long-contained, the often-imitated, but never duplicated … Genie of the Lamp.' This string of quotable noun phrases leads into the seductively rhyming invitation, 'Why don't you ruminate, whilst I illuminate?'

It might be worth us taking a moment to ruminate about new narratives as we negotiate this period of transformation in reading. Children transform the texts they meet, mingling them to create their own meanings and using them as scaffolds for more adventurous texts. They adapt the models and examples available to them in a way which is illuminating for adults. Adults know that texts transform readers, adding to experience and growth in understanding. A little rumination might lead to a sense that if we are to model reading for children we need to develop ways of understanding and talking about new texts. We need to create a new community of reading experience. We need to remind ourselves that we already know some of the languages of texts as well as learning to communicate even more widely with the heteroglossia of texts. We need to re-appraise just how we map out the pathways as we read. We need to learn how to

VERDICT

BENJI

Wow what a game if you think this is dull you must be mad. The graphics are brilliant it's one of the best snes games alive. You firally get a chance to be Bowser in a platformer also the 2 player system allows you to to fight in a kind of beat'emup style donkey v.s Bowser?or mario vs Luigi whoever you choose We Cove this and recomend it for you.

ATTENTION MORTAL WHO IS READING THIS REVIEW BUY THIS GAME.

Figure 13.2

negotiate the sometimes daunting terrain of multimodal and multimedia texts, accompanying young readers as they explore new territory. Can we afford to let them make those journeys alone?

NOTES AND REFERENCES

1. These figures come from research carried out by the author as part of a project looking at children's production of multimodal texts.
2. I am grateful to Sally Wilkinson, advisory teacher for English in Suffolk, for Darryl's text.

Alexie, S. (1997) *Indian Killer*. London: Vintage.

Arnold, M. (1861) 'Democracy', in Super, R.H. (ed.) *Complete Prose Works of Matthew Arnold* (1962, revised edition). Ann Arbor: University of Michigan Press.

Bain, R. (1999) 'ICT 4 English: hyper-texting', in *The Secondary English Magazine*, Vol. 2, no. 3.

Bakhtin, M. (1981), in Holquist, M. (ed.) *The Dialogic Imagination*. Texas: University of Texas Press.

Bearne, E. (1996) 'Mind the Gap: critical literacy as a dangerous underground movement', in Styles, M., Bearne, E. and Watson, V. (eds.) *Voices Off: Texts, Contexts and Readers*. London: Cassell.

Browne, A. (1997) 'Never too old for picture books', *Times Educational Supplement*, 15 December 1997.

Fenwick, G. (1998) 'The Beano-Dandy Phenomenon' in Evans, J. (ed.) *What's in the Picture? Responding to Illustrations in Picture Books*. London: Paul Chapman Publishing.

Halliday, M. (1985) *An Introduction to Functional Grammar*. London: Edward Arnold.

Kress, G. (1997) *Before Writing: rethinking the paths to literacy*. London: Routledge.

Kress, G. and van Leeuwen T. (1996) *The Grammar of Visual Design*. London: Routledge.

Newbery, J., in Harvey Darton, F.J. (1932) *Children's Books in England*. Cambridge: Cambridge University Press.

Parker, D. (1999) 'You've read the Book, Now Make the Film', in *English in Education*, Vol. 33, no. 1. Sheffield: NATE.

Pullman, P. (1989) *Spring-Heeled Jack a story of bravery and evil*. London: Corgi Yearling Books.

Richards, M. (1998) 'Back to School', in *PC Guide*, Vol. 4, Issue 6.

Robinson, J. and Estes, J. (1996) *Batman/Deadman: death and glory*. New York: DC Comics.

Rowe, A.(1996) 'Reading Wordless Picture Books', in Styles, M., Bearne, E. and Watson, V. (eds.) *Voices Off: Texts, Contexts and Readers*. London: Cassell.

Sanger, J., Willson, J., Davies, B., Whitaker, R. (1997) *Young Children, Videos and Computer Games: issues for teachers and parents*. London: Falmer Press.

Spratt, N. and Sturdy, R. (1998) 'Reading and Gender', in Bearne, E. (ed.) *Use of Language Across the Secondary Curriculum*. London: Routledge.

Townsend, J.R. (1996) 'Parents and Children' in Styles, M., Bearne, E. and Watson, V. (eds) *Voices Off: Texts, Contexts and Readers*. London: Cassell.

Williams, R. (1958) *Culture and Society*. Harmondsworth: Penguin.

Name Index

Subject Index